Essential

Arabic

phrase book

Compiled by
Fethi Mansouri

PERIPLUS

Published by Periplus Editions (HK) Ltd. with editorial offices at
364 Innovation Drive, North Clarendon, Vermont 05759 U.S.A.
and 130 Joo Seng Road #06-01, Singapore 368357.

LCC Card No. 2003112388
ISBN-13: 978-0-7946-0184-3
ISBN-10: 0-7946-0184-7

Distributed by:

Asia Pacific
Berkeley Books Pte. Ltd.
130 Joo Seng Road #06-01
Singapore 368357
Tel: (65) 6280-1330
Fax: (65) 6280-6290
inquiries@periplus.com.sg
www.periplus.com

North America, Latin America & Europe
Tuttle Publishing
364 Innovation Drive
North Clarendon, VT 05759-9436 U.S.A.
Tel: 1 (802) 773-8930
Fax: 1 (802) 773-6993
info@tuttlepublishing.com
www.tuttlepublishing.com

Japan
Tuttle Publishing
Yaekari Building, 3rd Floor
5-4-12 Osaki
Shinagawa-ku
Tokyo 141-0032
Tel: (81) 3 5437-0171
Fax: (81) 3 5437-0755
tuttle-sales@gol.com

Indonesia
PT Java Books Indonesia
Kawasan Industri Pulogadung
Jl. Rawa Gelam IV No. 9
Jakarta 13930
Tel: (62) 21 4682-1088
Fax: (62) 21 461-0207
cs@javabooks.co.id

11 10 09 08 07   8 7 6 5 4 3

Printed in Singapore

Contents

Introduction

• **Welcome to the new Periplus Essential Phrase Books series, covering the world's most popular languages and containing everything you'd expect from a comprehensive language series. They're concise, accessible and easy to understand, and youíll find them indispensable on your trip abroad.**

Each guide is divided into 15 themed sections and starts with a pronunciation guide which explains the phonetic pronunciation to all the words and phrases you'll need to know for your trip, while at the back of the book is an extensive word list and grammar guide which will help you construct basic sentences in your chosen language.

Throughout the book you'll come across colored boxes with a ⬤ beside them. These are designed to help you if you can't understand what your listener is saying to you. Hand the book over to them and encourage them to point to the appropriate answer to the question you are asking.

Other colored boxes in the book — this time without the symbol — give listings of themed words with their English translations beside them.

For extra clarity, we have put all English words and phrases in **black**, foreign language terms in **red**, followed by their phonetic pronunciation.

This phrase book covers all subjects you are likely to come across during the course of your visit, from reserving a room for the night to ordering food and drink at a restaurant and what to do if your car breaks down or you lose your traveler's checks and money. With over 2,000 commonly used words and essential phrases at your fingertips you can rest assured that you will be able to get by in all situations, so let the Essential Phrase Book become your passport to a secure and enjoyable trip!

Pronunciation guide

The imitated pronunciation should be read as if it were English, bearing in mind that the emphatic consonants indicate more a vowel volume than a separate sound.

English	Arabic	Phonetic Description	Approximate in English
b	ب	voiced labial stop	b as in bad
d	د	voiced alveolar stop	as in dad
d	ض	emphatic voiced alveolar stop	does not exist (similar to Don)
f	ف	voiceless labio-dental fricative	as in fat
h	ه	voiceless glottal fricative	as in hat
h	ح	voiceless pharyngeal fricative	does not exist
j	ج	voiced palato-alveolar fricative	as in jelly
k	ك	voiceless velar stop	as in kick
l	ل	alveolar lateral	as in lick
m	م	bilabial nasal	as in might
n	ن	alveolar nasal	as in night
q	ق	uvular stop	does not exist
r	ر	alveolar trill	as in right
s	س	voiceless alveolar fricative	as in sight
s	ص	emphatic voiceless alveolar fricative	does not exist (similar to Sahara)
t	ت	voiceless dental fricative	as in tight
t	ط	emphatic voiceless alveolar stop	does not exist (similar to Tokyo)
z	ز	voiced alveolar fricative	as in zebra
z	ظ	emphatic voiced alveolar fricative	dh or z (depends on region)
'	أ، ء	glottal stop	a
`	ع	voiced pharyngeal fricative	does not exist
sh	ش	voiceless palato-alveolar fricative	as in shoes
th	ث	voiceless dental fricative	as in three
dh	ذ	voiced dental fricative	as in there
kh	خ	voiceless velar fricative	does not exist
gh	غ	voiced velar fricative	does not exist
y	ي	palatal glide	as in yellow
w	و	bilabial approximant	as in wall

Vowels: there are three basic short vowels in Arabic and three long ones. These are:

Vowel	Phonetic description	English equivalent
a	short low back vowel	as in **A**msterdam
aa	long low back vowel	as in *far*
i	short high front vowel	as in *inside*
ii	long high front vowel	as in *clean*
u	short high back vowel	as in *to go*
uu	long high back vowel	as in *noon*

Stressing of words

Arabic words do not have a stressed syllable in the manner that English words do. However, individual consonants can exhibit stress by means of a *shadda* (gemination)—this is represented by a duplicated consonant. For example, in the word **kassara** "to break," the duplicated s indicates consonantal stress as in the English name *Cassandra*.

Useful lists

Useful lists

1.1 **T**oday or tomorrow?

What day is it today? _____	ما اليوم؟
	maa l-yawm?
Today's Monday _____	اليوم الإثنين
	al-yawm al-'ithnayn
Tuesday _____	الثلاثاء
	ath-thulaathaa'
Wednesday _____	ألاربعاء
	al-'arbi aa'
Thursday _____	الخميس
	al-khamiis
Friday _____	الجمعة
	al-jumu'a
Saturday _____	السبت
	as-sabt
Sunday_____	الاحد
	al-'ahad
in January _____	في كانون الثاني
	fii kaanuun ath-thaanii
since February _____	منذ شهر شباط
	mundhu shahr shubaat
in spring _____	في الربيع
	fii ar-rabii'
in summer _____	في الصيف
	fii as-sayf
in autumn _____	في الخريف
	fii al-khariif
in winter _____	في الشتاء
	fii ash-shitaa'
2001 _____	الفان وواحد
	alfaan wa waahid
the twentieth century _____	القرن العشرون
	al-qarnu al-'ishruun
the twenty-first century ____	القرن الحادي والعشرون
	al-qarnu al-haadii wa al-'ishruun
What's the date today? _____	ما هو التاريخ اليوم؟
	maa huwa taariikhu al-yawm?

Today's the twenty-fourth ___	اليوم هو الرابع والعشرون al-yawm huwa ar-raabi' wa al-'ishruun
Monday 3 November _____	الإثنين ثلاث تشرين الثاني al-ithnayn thalaatha tishriin ath-thaanii
in the morning _____	في الصباح fii as-sabaah
in the afternoon _____	بعد الظهر ba'da az-zuhr
in the evening _____	في المساء fii al-masaa'
at night _____	في الليل fii al-layl
this morning _____	هذا الصباح haadhaa as-sabaah
this afternoon _____	بعد ظهر اليوم ba'da zuhr al-yawm
this evening _____	هذا المساء haadhaa al-masaa'
tonight _____	هذه الليلة haadhihi al-layla
last night _____	البارحة al-baariha
this week _____	هذا الاسبوع haadhaa al-usbuu'
next month _____	الشهر القادم ash-shahr al-qaadim
last year _____	السنة الماضية as-sana al-maadiya
next... _____	القادم al-qaadim
in...days / weeks / months / __ years	خلال... ايام/اسابيع/اشهر/سنين khilaal...ayyaam / asaabii' / ashhur / siniin
weeks ago _____	منذ اسابيع mundhu asaabii'
day off _____	يوم إجازة yawm ijaaza

.2 Legal holidays

Please note that for Islamic religious holidays, the dates change from one year to another because the Muslim / lunar calendar is ten days shorter than the Christian calendar (used throughout the world). The dates listed for the Islamic holidays are for the year 2003. The most important legal holidays in the Middle East are the following:

January 1	New Year's Day
	١ كانون الثاني يوم رأس السنة
	al-awwal min kaanuun ath-thaanii yawm ra's as-sana

February 12	Eid Ul-idh-ha (Festival of Sacrifice)
	١٢ عيد الإضحى/ الثاني عشر من شباط
	athaanii 'ashar min shubaat / 'idul idh-ha

March/April	Easter and Easter Monday
	نيسان/آذار عيد الفصح و اثنين الفصح
	nisaan/aadhar 'iid al-fish wa ithnayn al-fish

March 5	Islamic New Year (Hijra)
	٥ آذار رأس السنة الهجرية
	al-khaamis min aadhaar, ra's s-sana al-hijriyya

1 May	Labor Day
	١ أيار عيد العمال
	al-awwal min ayaar 'iid al-'ummaal

27 October	Beginning of Ramadan (Islamic holy month of fasting)
	٢٧ تشرين أول رمضان
	sab'a wa 'ishriin tishriin 'awwal, ramadhaan

26 November	Eid al-Fitr (End of Ramadan)
	٢٦ تشرين الثاني عيد الفطر
	sitta wa 'ishriin tishriin ath-thaanii 'iidu l-fitr

25 December	Christmas Day
	٢٥ كانون الاول عيد الميلاد
	khamsa wa 'ishriin kaanuun al-awwal 'iidu l-miilaad

Most shops, banks and government institutions are closed on these days. Individual towns also have public holidays to celebrate their own patron saints.

.3 What time is it?

| What time is it? _____ | كم الساعة الان؟ |
| | kam as-saa'a al'aan? |

| It's nine o'clock _____ | الساعة التاسعة |
| | as-saa'a at-taasi'a |

| - five past ten _____ | العاشرة وخمس دقائق |
| | al-'aashira wa khams daqaa'iq |

- a quarter past eleven _____ الحادية عشرة والربع
al-haadiya 'ashra wa ar-rub'

- twenty past twelve _____ الثانية عشرة والثلث (وعشرون دقيقة)
ath-thaaniya 'ashara wa ath-thulth
('ishruun daqiiqa)

- half past one _____ الواحدة والنصف
al-waahida wa an-nisf

- twenty-five to three _____ الثانية وخمسة وثلاثون دقيقة
ath-thaaniya wa khamsa wa
thalaathuun daqiiqa

- a quarter to four _____ الرابعة الاربعا
ar-raabi'a illaa rubu'an

- ten to five _____ الخامسة إلا عشر دقائق
al-khaamisa illaa 'ashr daqaa'iq

It's midday (twelve noon) _____ منتصف النهار
muntasafu an-nahaar

It's midnight _____ منتصف الليل
muntasafu al-layl

half an hour _____ نصف ساعة
nisf saa'a

What time? _____ متى؟
mataa?

What time can I come by? _____ متى استطيع ان آتي؟
mtaa astatii' an a'tii?

At... _____ عند . . .
'inda...

After... _____ بعد . . .
ba'da...

Before... _____ قبل . . .
qabla...

Between...and... _____ بين الساعة . . .و . . .
bayna as-saa'a...wa...

From...to... _____ من . . .الى . . .
min...ilaa...

In...minutes _____ خلال . . .دقائق
khilaal...daqaa'iq

- an hour _____ ساعة واحدة
saa'a waahida

- ...hours _____ ساعات . . .
...saa'aat

- a quarter of an hour _____ ربع ساعة
rub'u saa'a

- three quarters of an hour ___ ثلاثة ارباع الساعة
thalaathat arbaa' as-saa'a

too early / late _____ متأخر / مبكرا كثيرا
muta'akhir / mubakkiran kathiiran

on time _____ في الموعد تماما
fii alwaw'id tamaaman

summertime _____ التوقيت الصيفي
(daylight saving) at-tawqiit as-sayfii

wintertime _____ التوقيت الشتوي
at-tawqiit ash-shitwii

1 .4 One, two, three...

0 _____ صفر
sifr

1 _____ واحد
waahid

2 _____ اثنان
ithnaan

3 _____ ثلاثة
thalaatha

4 _____ اربعة
arba'a

5 _____ خمسة
khamsa

6 _____ ستة
sitta

7 _____ سبعة
sab'a

8 _____ ثمانية
thamaaniya

9 _____ تسعة
tis'a

10 _____ عشرة
'ashara

11 _____ احد عشر
ahada 'ashar

12 _____ اثنى عشر
ithnay 'ashara

13	_____	ثلاثة عشر thalaathata 'ashara
14	_____	اربعة عشر arba'ata 'ashara
15	_____	خمسة عشر khamsat 'ashara
16	_____	ستة عشر sittaat 'ashara
17	_____	سبعة عشر sab'ata 'ashara
18	_____	ثمانية عشر thamaaniyata 'ashara
19	_____	تسعة عشر tis'ata 'ashara
20	_____	عشرون 'ishruun
21	_____	واحد وعشرون waahid wa 'ishruun
22	_____	اثنان وعشرون ithnaan wa 'ishruun
30	_____	ثلاثون thalaathuun
31	_____	واحد وثلاثون waahid wa thalaathuun
32	_____	اثنان وثلاثون ithnaan wa thalaathuun
40	_____	اربعون arba'uun
50	_____	خمسون khamsuun
60	_____	ستون sittuun
70	_____	سبعون sab'uun
80	_____	ثمانون thamaanuun
90	_____	تسعون tis'uun
100	_____	مئة mi'a

101	_____	مئة وواحد mi'a wa waahid
110	_____	مئة وعشرة mi'a wa 'ashara
120	_____	مئة عشرون mi'a wa 'ishruun
200	_____	متتان mi'ataan
300	_____	ثلاثمئة thalaathumi'a
400	_____	اربعمئة arba'umi'a
500	_____	خمسمئة khamsumi'a
600	_____	ستمئة sittumi'a
700	_____	سبعمئة sab'umi'a
800	_____	ثمانمئة thamaanimi'a
900	_____	تسعمئة tis'umi'a
1,000	_____	الف 'alf
1,100	_____	الف ومئة 'alf wa mi'a
2,000	_____	الفان 'alfaan
10,000	_____	عشرة الاف 'ashrat 'alaaf
100,000	_____	مئة الف mi'at 'alf
1,000,000	_____	مليون malyuun
1st	_____	الاول al-awwal
2nd	_____	الثاني ath-thaanii
3rd	_____	الثالث ath-thaalith

4th	_____	الرابع
		ar-raabi'
5th	_____	الخامس
		al-khaamis
6th	_____	السادس
		as-saadis
7th	_____	السابع
		as-saabi'
8th	_____	الثامن
		ath-thaamin
9th	_____	التاسع
		at-taasi'
10th	_____	العاشر
		al-'aashir
11th	_____	الحادي عشر
		al-haadii 'ashar
12th	_____	الثاني عشر
		ath-thaanii 'ashar
13th	_____	الثالث عشر
		ath-thaalith 'ashar
14th	_____	الرابع عشر
		ar-rabi' 'ashar
15th	_____	الخامس عشر
		al-khaamis 'ashar
16th	_____	السادس عشر
		as-saadis 'ashar
17th	_____	السابع عشر
		as-saabi' 'ashar
18th	_____	الثامن عشر
		ath-thamin 'ashar
19th	_____	التاسع عشر
		at-taasi' 'ashar
20th	_____	العشرون
		al-'ishruun
21st	_____	الحادي والعشرون
		al-haadii wa al-'ishruun
22nd	_____	الثاني والعشرون
		ath-thaanii wa al-'ishruun
30th	_____	الثلاثون
		ath-thalaathuun

100th	المئة	al-mi'a
1,000th	الالف	al-'alf
once	مرة واحد	marra waahida
twice	مرتين	marratayn
double	ضعف	di'f
triple	ثلاثة اضعاف	thalaathat ad'aaf
half	نصف	nisf
a quarter	ربع	rub'
a third	ثلث	thuluth
some / a few	بعض / بضع	ba'd / bid'u
2 + 4 = 6	اثنين زائد اربعة يساوي ستة	ithnayn zaa'id arba'a yusaawii sitta
4 – 2 = 2	اربعة ناقص اثنين يساوي اثنين	arba'a naaqis ithnayn yusaawii ithnayn
2 x 4 = 8	اربعة ضارب اثنين يساوي ثمانية	arba'a daarib ithnayn yusaawii thamaaniya
4 ÷ 2 = 2	اربعة على اثنين يساوي اثنين	arba'a 'alaa ithnayn yusaawii ithnayn
even / odd	فردي / زوجي	fardiy / zawjiy
total	مجموع	majmuu'
6 x 9	تسعة ضارب ستة	tis'a daarib sitta

1 .5 The weather

Is the weather going to be good / bad?	هل سيكون الطقس جيدا / سيئا ؟ hal sayakuun at-taqs jayyid / sayyi'?

Is it going to get colder / hotter?	هل سيكون الطقس ابرد /احر ؟ hal sayakuun at-taqs abrad / ahar?
What temperature is it going to be?	كيف ستكون درجة الحرارة ؟ kayfa satakuun darajatu l-haraara?
Is it going to rain?	هل ستمطر ؟ hal satumtir?
Is there going to be a storm?	هل ستكون هناك عاصفة ؟ hal satakuun hunaaka 'aasifa?
Is it going to snow?	هل سيتساقط الثلج ؟ hal sayatasaaqat ath-thalj?
Is it going to freeze?	هل سيكون هناك تجلد ؟ hal sayakuunu hunaaka tajallud?
Is the thaw setting in?	هل ستذوب الثلوج ؟ hal satadhuub ath-thuluuj?
Is it going to be foggy?	هل سيكون هناك ضباب ؟ hal sayakuunu hunaaka dabaab?
Is there going to be a thunderstorm?	هل ستكون هناك عواصف رعدية ؟ hal satakuun hunaaka 'awaasif ra'diyya?
The weather's changing	الطقس متغير /متقلب at-taqs mutaghayyir (mutaqallib)
It's going to be cold	سيكون الطقس باردا sayakuunu at-taqs baaridan
What's the weather going to be like today / tomorrow?	كيف سيكون الطقس اليوم/ غدا ؟ kayfa sayakuunu at-taqs al-yawm / ghadan?

حر شديد جدا /رطب har shadiid jiddan / ratib **sweltering / muggy**	صقيع saqii' **frost**	مطر matar **rain**
مشمس mushmis **sunny**	صقيع في الليل saqii' fii l-layl **overnight frost**	عصفة ريح 'asfat riih **gusts of wind**
جيد /حسن jayyid / hasan **fine**	جليد /ثلجي jaliid / thalj **ice / icy**	انهمار المطر inhimaar al-matar **downpour**
تجمد /متجمد tajammud / mutajammid **frost / frosty**	يوم مشمس yawmun mushmis **sunny day**	سماء صافية/غائمة samaa' saafiya / ghaa'ima **clear skies / cloudy**

صافي / صحو	...درجات فوق / تحت	حار جدا
saafi / sahw	الصفر	haar jiddan
fine / clear	...darajaat fawqa / tahta as-sifr	very hot
خانق	...degrees below / above zero	مطر غزيز
khaaniq		matar ghaziir
stifling	برد	heavy rain
عاصفة	barad	رياح متوسطة السرعة /
'aasifa	hail	قوية / قوية جدا
storm	لطيف	riyaah mutawassitat as-sur'a / qawiyya / qawiyya jidan
رطب	latiif	moderate / strong / very strong winds
ratib	mild	
humid	ضباب / ضبابي	بارد ورطب
إعصار	dabaab / dabaabi	baarid wa ratib
i'saar	fog / foggy	cold and damp
hurricane	ثلج	بارد
رياح	thalj	baarid
riyaah	snow	cool
wind	غائم	مكشوف
	ghaa'im	makshuuf
	cloudiness	bleak
	موجة حر	عاصف
	mawjat har	'aasif
	heatwave	windy

1.6 Here, there

See also 5.1 Asking for directions

here / there	هنا / هناك hunaa / hunaak
somewhere / nowhere	في مكان ما / غير موجود fii makaanin maa / ghayr mawjuud
everywhere	في كل مكان fii kul makaan
far away / nearby	بعيد / قريب ba'iid / qariib
(on the) right / (on the) left	على اليمين / اليسار 'alaa al-yamiin / al-yasaar
to the right / left of...	الى يمين / يسار الـ... ilaa yamiin / yasaar al-...

Useful lists

straight ahead	مباشرة	mubaa<u>sh</u>aratan
via	عن طريق	'an <u>t</u>ariiq
in / to	في /الى	fii / ilaa
on	على	'alaa
under	تحت	ta<u>h</u>ta
against	عكس	'aks
opposite / facing	مقابل/مواجه	muqaabil / muwaajih
next to	بالقرب من	bil-qurbi min
near	قرب	qurba
in front of	امام	amaama
in the center	في المركز	fii al-markaz
forward	إلى الامام	ilaa al-amaam
down	اسفل	asfal
up	فوق/اعلى	a'laa / fawq
inside	داخل	daa<u>kh</u>il
outside	خارج	<u>kh</u>aarij
behind	خلف	<u>kh</u>alf
at the front	في الامام	fii al-amaam
at the back / in line	الى الوراء/في الصف	ilaa al-waraa' / fii a<u>s</u>-<u>s</u>affi
in the north	في الشمال	fii a<u>sh</u>-<u>sh</u>amaal

to the south	الى الجنوب ilaa al-januub
from the west	من الغرب min al-gharb
from the east	من الشرق min ash-sharq
to the...of	الى الـ...من ilaa al-...min

1.7 What does the sign say?

See 5.4 Traffic signs

للإيجار
lil'iijaar
for hire

ماء حار/بارد
maa' haar / baarid
hot / cold water

ماء صالح/غير صالح الشرب
maa' saalih / ghayr saalih lish-shurb
no drinking water

للإيجار
lil'iijaar
for rent

فندق
funduq
hotel

قف
qif
stop

قوة كهربائية عالية
quwwa kahrabaa-'iyya 'aaliya
high voltage

مفتوح
maftuuh
open

إحذر الكلاب
ihdhar al-kilaab
beware of the dog

نافذ
naafidh
sold out

توقف اضطراري
tawaqquf idtiraari
emergency brake

غير قابل للاستعمال
ghayr qaabil lil'isti'maal
not in use

غرفة الحمام
ghurfat al-hammam
bathroom

عاطل
'aatil
out of order

للبيع
lil-bay'
for sale

معلومات
ma'luumaat
information

اجرة الدخول
ujrat ad-dukhuul
entrance (free)

الرجاء عدم الإزعاج اللمس
ar-rajaa' 'adam l-iz'aaj l-lamas
please do not disturb

غرفة انتظار
ghurfat intizaar
waiting room

مهرب من الحريق/سلم ميكانيكي
mahrab min al-hariiq / sullam miikaaniikii
fire escape / escalator

ادفع
idfa'
push

اسحب
ishab
pull

مكتب معلومات السياح
maktab ma'luumaat as-suyaah
tourist information bureau

مكتب البريد
maktab bariid
post office

مخرج طوارىء
makhraj tawaari'
(emergency) exit

دهن طري
duhn tarii
wet paint

Useful lists

خطر
khaṭar
danger

مكتب تذاكر سفر
maktab tadhaakir safar
ticket office

شرطة
shurṭa
police

تصريف
taṣriif
exchange

محاسب/امين الصندوق
muhaasib / amiin aṣ-ṣunduuq
cashier

مغلق
mughlaq
closed (for holiday / refurbishment)

مملوء
mamluu'
full

مشغول
mashghuul
engaged

جدول مواعيد
jadwal mawaa'iid
timetable

مستشفى
mustashfaa
hospital

مشاة
mushaat
pedestrians

خطر / خطر حريق / خطر على حياتك
khaṭar / khaṭar hariiq / khaṭar 'alaa hayaatik
danger / fire hazard / danger to life

شرطة المرور
shurṭat al-muruur
traffic police

ممنوع الصيد
mamnuu' aṣ-ṣayd
no hunting / fishing

ممنوع التدخين/لا ترم المهملات
mamnuu' at-tadkhiin / laa tarmi al-muhmalaat
no smoking / no litter

ممنوع الدخول
mamnuu' ad-dukhuul
no entry

قسم الاطفاء
qism al-iṭfaa'
fire department

شرطة/البلدية
shurṭa / al-baladiyya
(municipal) police

محجوز
mahjuuz
reserved

اسعافات اولية/ حادث وطوارىء
is'aafat awwaliyya / haadith wa ṭawaari'
first aid / accident and emergency (hospital)

مدخل
madkhal
entrance

1.8 Telephone alphabets

Pronouncing the alphabets:

b	——	ب	ba
d	——	د	dal
d̠	——	ض	d̠ad
f	——	ف	faa'
h	——	ه	haa'
h̠	——	ح	h̠aa'
j	——	ج	jiim
k	——	ك	kaaf
l	——	ل	laam

m	م	miim
n	ن	nuun
q	ق	qaaf
r	ر	raa'
s	س	siin
<u>s</u>	ص	<u>s</u>aad
t	ت	taa'
<u>t</u>	ط	<u>t</u>aa'
z	ز	zayn
<u>z</u>	ظ	<u>z</u>aa'
'	ء	hamza
	ع	ayn
<u>sh</u>	ش	<u>sh</u>iin
<u>th</u>	ث	<u>th</u>aa'
<u>dh</u>	ذ	<u>dh</u>aal
<u>kh</u>	خ	<u>kh</u>aa'
<u>gh</u>	غ	<u>gh</u>ayn
y	ي	yaa'
w	و	waaw

Vowels

a	ا	fatha
i	ي	kasra
u	و	damma

1.9 Personal details

surname	اللقب/اسم العائلة al-laqab / ism al-'aa'ila
first name	الاسم al-ism
initials	مختصر الإسم mu<u>kh</u>ta<u>s</u>ar al-ism
address (street / number)	العنوان/إسم ورقم الشارع al-'unwaan / ism wa raqam a<u>sh</u>-<u>sh</u>aari'
postal (zip) code / town	المدينة/الرقم البريدي ar-raqm al-bariidi / al-madiina

| sex (male / female) _____ | الجنس (ذكر / انثى) |
| | al-jins (dhakar / unthaa) |

nationality _____ الجنسية
al-jinsiyya

date of birth _____ تاريخ الولادة
taariikh al-wilaada

place of birth _____ مكان الولادة
makaan al-wilaada

occupation _____ المهنة
al-mihna

marital status _____ الحالة المدنية
al-haala al-madaniyya

married / single _____ متزوج/اعزب
mutazawwij / a'zab

widowed _____ أرملة
armala

(number of) children _____ عدد الاطفال
'adad al-atfaal

passport / identity card / ____ جواز سفر/بطاقة شخصية/رقم رخصة
driving license number السياقة
jawaaz safar / bitaaqa shakhsiyya /
raqam rukhsat as-siyaaqa

place and date of issue ____ محل وتاريخ الصدور
mahal wa taariikh as-suduur

signature _____ التوقيع
at-tawqii'

Courtesies

2 Courtesies

* It is common in the Arab countries for men to shake hands on meeting and parting company. However, for religious and cultural reasons some women might not feel comfortable shaking hands with male strangers. Female friends and relatives may kiss each other on both cheeks when meeting and parting company. For men, this is also quite usual. When addressing men and women the terms **sayyid** and **sayyida** (meaning "Mr" and "Ms") are often used in more formal situations while **akh** and **ukht** (meaning "brother" and "sister") are used in more casual informal contexts.

2.1 Greetings

Hello / Good morning, Mr Williams
أهلا/صباح الخير سيد وليام
ahlan / sabaahu al-khayr sayyid wilyamz

Hello / Good morning, Mrs Jones
أهلا/صباح الخير سيدة جونز
ahlan / sabaahu al-khayr sayyida jonz

Hello, Peter
أهلا بيتر
ahlan biitar

Hi, Helen
أهلا هيلين
ahlan hiiliin

Good morning, madam
صباح الخير مدام
sabaahu al-khayr madaam

Good afternoon, sir
مساء الخير سيد
masaa'u al-khay sayyid

Good afternoon / evening
أهلا/مساء الخير
ahlan / masaa'u al-khayr

Hello / Good morning
أهلا/صباح الخير
ahlan / sabaahu al-khayr

How are you? / How are things?
كيف حالك؟/كيف امورك؟
kayfa haaluk? / kayfa umuuruk?

Fine, thank you, and you?
بخير، شكرا، وأنت؟
bikhayr, shukran, wa anta?

Very well, and you?
جيد جدا، وانت؟
jayyid jiddan, wa anta?

In excellent health / In great shape
في صحة ممتازة/في حالة ممتازة
fii sihha mumtaaza / fii haala mumtaaza

So-so
لابأس
laa ba's

Not very well
لست على ما يرام
lastu 'alaa maa yuraam

Not bad _____	لا بأس laa ba'sa
I'm going to leave _____	أنا على وشك ان اغادر anaa 'alaa washak an ughaadir
I have to be going, _____ someone's waiting for me	يجب ان اذهب الآن، شخص ما ينتظرني yajib an adhhaba al'aan shakhsun maa yantazirunii
Goodbye _____	مع السلامة ma'a s-salaama
See you later _____	أراك فيما بعد araaka fiimaa ba'd
See you soon _____	أراك قريبا araaka qariiban
See you in a little while _____	أراك بعد حين araaka ba'da hiin
Sweet dreams _____	احلام سعيدة ahlaam sa'iida
Good night _____	تصبح على خير tusbih 'ala khayr
All the best _____	أتمنى لك كل خير atamanna laka kulla khayr
Have fun _____	ارجو ان تتسلى جيدا arjuu an tatasallaa jayyidan
Good luck _____	حظا سعيدا hazzan sa'iidan
Have a nice vacation _____	أتمنى لك أجازة سعيدة atamanaa laka ijaaza sa'iida
Have a good trip _____	أتمنى لك رحلة ممتعة atamanna laka rihla mumti'a
Thank you, the same _____ to you	شكرا، وانت كذلك shukran, wa anta kadhalika
Give my regards to... _____ (formal)	بلغ تحياتي لـ... balligh tahiyyaatii lii...
Say hello to...(informal) _____	سلم على... sallim 'alaa...

2.2 How to ask a question

Who? _____	من؟ man?

Who's that? / Who is it? / ____ Who's there?	من ذلك؟ /من هو؟ /من هناك؟ man dhaalik? / man huwa? / man hunaak?
What? ____	ماذا؟ maadhaa?
What is there to see? ____	ماذا هناك لنرى؟ maadhaa hunaaka linaraa?
What category of hotel is it?__	مانوع (درجة) هذا الفندق؟ maa naw' (darajat)haadhaa al-fundiq?
Where? ____	اين؟ ayna?
Where's the bathroom? ____	اين غرفة الحمام؟ ayna ghurfatu al-hammaam?
Where are you going? ____	إلى أين انت ذاهب؟ ilaa ayna anta dhaahib?
Where are you from? ____	من أي بلد انت؟ min ayyi balad anta?
What? / How? ____	ماذا؟ /كيف؟ maadhaa / kayfa?
How far is that? ____	كم يبعد ذلك؟ kam ya'bud dhaalik?
How long does that take? ____	كم سيستغرق ذلك؟ kam sa-yastaghriq dhaalik?
How long is the trip? ____	كم ستستغرق الرحلة؟ kam sa-tastaghriq ar-rihla?
How much? ____	كم؟ kam?
How much is this? ____	كم سعر هذا؟ kam si'ru haadhaa?
What time is it? ____	كم الوقت الأن؟ kam al-waqtu al-aan?
Which one(s)? ____	أي واحد /أي؟ ay waahid / ay...?
Which glass is mine? ____	أي كأس لي؟ ay ka'sin lii?
When? ____	متى؟ mataa?
When are you leaving? ____	متى ستغادر؟ mataa sa-tughaadir?

Why?	لماذا؟ limaadhaa?
Could you...?	هل يمكن...من فضلك؟ hal yumkin...min fadlik?
Could you help me, please?	هل يمكن ان تساعدني من فضلك؟ hal yumkin an tusaa'idani min fadlik?
Could you point that out to me / show me, please?	هل يمكن ان تبين لى ذلك/تريني ذلك من فضلك؟ hal yumkin an tubayyina lii dhaalika / turiyanii dhaalik min fadlik?
Could you come with me, please?	هل يمكن ان تأتي معي من فضلك؟ hal yumkin an ta'tiya ma'ii min fadlik?
Could you book me some tickets, please?	هل يمكن ان تحجز لي تذاكر سفر من فضلك؟ hal yumkin tahjiza lii tadhaakira safar min fadlik?
Could you recommend another hotel?	هل تنصحني بفندق آخر؟ hal tansahunii bi-funduq aakhar?
Do you know...?	من فضلك، هل تعرف...؟ min fadlik, hal ta'rif...?
Do you know whether...?	هل تعرف إذا كان...؟ hal ta'rif idhaa kaana...?
Do you have...?	هل لديكم...؟ hal ladaykum...?
Do you have a...for me?	هل لديك...لي؟ hal ladayka...lii?
Do you have a vegetarian dish, please?	هل لديك طبق خضروات من فضلك؟ hal ladayka tabaq khudrawaat min fadlik?
I would like...	اريد... uriidu...
I'd like a kilo of apples, please	اريد كيلو تفاح من فضلك uriidu kiilu tuffaah min fadlik
May I?	هل يمكنني أن؟ hal yumkinuni an?
May I take this away?	هل يمكن ان أسلك هذ الطريق؟ hal yumkin an asluka haadhaa at-tariiq?
Can I smoke here?	هل يمكن ان ادخن هنا؟ hal yumkin an udakhina hunaa?

Could I ask you something? ___ هل يمكن ان أسالك سؤال؟
hal yumkin an as'alaka su'aalan?

2.3 How to reply

Yes, of course _____ نعم، طبعا
na'am, tab'an

No, I'm sorry _____ لا، انا آسف
laa, anaa aasif

Yes, what can I do for you? ___ نعم، هل من خدمة أقدمها لك؟
na'am, hal min khidma uqaddimuhaa
laka?

Just a moment, please _____ لحظة، من فضلك
lahza min fadlik

No, I don't have time now ___ كلا، ليس لدي الوقت الان
kallaa, laysa ladayya al-waqtu al-aan

No, that's impossible _____ لا، هذا مستحيل
laa, haadhaa mustahiil

I think so / I think that's   اظن كذلك/اظن ذلك صحيحا قطعا
absolutely right   azun kadhaalik / azunnu dhaalika
                                   sahihan qat'an

I think so too / I agree _____ أنا ايضا اظن كذلك/او افقك
anaa aydan azun kadhaalik / uwaafiquk

I hope so too _____ أتمنى ان يكون كذلك
atamannaa an yakuuna kadhaalik

No, not at all / Absolutely ___ لا، ليس كذلك/قطعا لا
not   laa, laysa kadhaalik / qat'an laa

No, no one _____ لا، لا أحد
laa, laa ahad

No, nothing _____ لا، لا شيء
laa, laa shay'

That's right _____ هذا صحيح
haadhaa sahiih

Something's wrong _____ هناك مشكلة ما
hunaaka mushkila maa

I agree / I don't agree _____ انا اوافق/لا اوافق
anaa uwaafiq / laa uwaafiq

OK / it's fine _____ نعم/هذا جيد
na'am / haadhaa jayyid

All right _____ تمام
tamaam

| Perhaps | ربما |
| | rubbamaa |

| I don't know | لا أعرف |
| | laa a'rif |

2.4 Thank you

| Thank you | شكرا |
| | shukran |

| You're welcome | أهلا وسهلا بك |
| | ahlan wa sahlan bika |

| Thank you very much / Many thanks | شكرا كثيرا/جزيل كثيرا |
| | shukran kathiiran / jaziilu kathiiran |

| Very kind of you | هذا لطف منك |
| | hadhaa lutfun minka |

| My pleasure | بكل سرور |
| | bikulli suruur |

| I enjoyed it very much | استمتعت بذلك كثيرا |
| | istamta'tu bidhaalika kathiiran |

| Thank you for... | شكرا لك على... |
| | shukran laka 'alaa... |

| You shouldn't have / That was so kind of you | لم يكن يلزمك/كان ذلك لطفا منك |
| | lam yakun yalzamuk / kaana dhaalika lutfan minka |

| Don't mention it! | العفو |
| | al-'afw |

| That's all right | ليست مشكلة |
| | laysat mushkila |

2.5 Sorry

| Excuse me / pardon me / sorry | عفوا/ارجو المعذرة/آسف |
| | 'afwan / arjuu al-ma'dhira / aasif |

| Sorry, I didn't know that... | عفوا لم اكن اعرف أنه... |
| | 'afwan lam akun a'rifu annahu... |

| I do apologize | انا اعتذر |
| | anaa a'tadhir |

| I'm sorry | انا اسف |
| | anaa aasif |

| I didn't mean it / it was an accident | لم اكن اقصد ذلك/حصل ذلك صدفة |
| | lam akun aqsid dhaalik / hasala dhaalika sudfa |

That's all right / don't _____ كل شيء تمام/لا تهتم
worry about it   kullu <u>shay</u>' tamaam / laa tahtam

Never mind / forget it _____ لا تهتم/انس ذلك
laa tahtam / insa <u>dh</u>aalik

It could happen to anyone __ هذا يحدث لأي شخص
haa<u>dh</u>aa ya<u>h</u>duth li'ay <u>shakh</u>s

2.6 What do you think?

Which do you prefer / _____ أيا تفضل/تحب اكثر؟
like best?   ayyan tufa<u>dd</u>il / tu<u>h</u>ib ak<u>th</u>ar?

What do you think? _____ ما رأيك؟
maa ra'yuka?

Don't you like dancing? _____ ألا تحب أن ترقص؟
alaa tu<u>h</u>ib an taqu<u>s</u>?

I don't mind _____ لا يهم
laa yahum

Well done! _____ أحسنت صنعا
a<u>h</u>santa <u>s</u>un'an!

Not bad! _____ لا بأس
laa ba'sa!

Great / marvelous! _____ عظيم/رائع
'a<u>z</u>iim / raa'i'!

Wonderful! _____ رائع
raa'i'!

How lovely! _____ كم هذا جميل
kam haa<u>dh</u>aa jamiil!

I am pleased for you _____ انا مسرور بشأنك
anaa masrur bi-<u>sha</u>'nika

I'm (not) very happy/ _____ انا (غير) مسرور جدا/مبتهج لـ...
delighted to...   anaa (<u>gh</u>ayr) masruur jiddan /
mubtahij li...

It's really nice here! _____ إنه حقا مكان جميل
innahu <u>h</u>aqqan makaanun jamiil!

How nice! _____ كم هذا جميل
kam haa<u>dh</u>aa jamiil!

How nice for you! _____ هذا امر رائع بالنسبة لك
haa<u>dh</u>aa amrun raa'i' bin-nisbati laka!

I'm very happy with... _____ أنا لست سعيدا جدا بـ...
anaa lastu sa'iidan jiddan bi...

I'm glad that... _____	أنا مسرور انه...
	anaa masruurun annahu...
I'm having a great time _____	انني أتسلى كثيرا
	innanii atasallaa kathiiran
I can't wait till tomorrow/ _____ I'm looking forward to tomorrow	لا أستطيع ان انتظر الى الغد/اتطلع الى الغد
	laa astatii' an antazir ilaa al-ghad/ atattala' ilaa al-ghad
I hope it works out _____	أتمنى ان تسير الامور كما يجب
	atamanna an tasiira al'umuuru kamaa yajibu
How awful! _____	يا له من أمر كريه
	yaa lahu min amrin kariih
It's horrible! _____	إنه امر فظيع
	innahu amrun fazii'!
That's ridiculous! _____	هذا امر سخيف
	haadhaa amrun sakhiif!
That's terrible! _____	يا له من امر رهيب
	yaa lahu min amrin rahiib!
What a pity / shame! _____	يا للشفقة/يا للاسف
	yaa lash-shafaqa / yaa lal'asaf!
How disgusting! _____	يا له من امر مزعج
	yaa lahu min amrin muz'ij!
What nonsense / how silly! __	أي هراء هذا/يا له من سخف
	ayya huraa' haadhaa / yaa lahu min sukhf!
I don't like it / them _____	انا لا احبه/احبهم
	anaa laa uhibuhu / uhibbuhum
I'm bored to death _____	أشعر بملل شديد
	ash'ur bi-malal shadiid
I'm fed up _____	انا منزعج
	anaa munza'ij
This is no good _____	هذا ليس جيدا
	haadhaa laysa jayyidan
This is not what I expected __	ليس هذا ما توقعت
	laysa haadhaa maa tawaqqa't

2

Courtesies

Conversation

3 Conversation

3.1 I beg your pardon?

I don't speak any Arabic / ___
I speak a little Arabic

انا لا أتكلم العربية كثيرا/انا أتكلم
العربية قليلا

anaa laa atakallamu al-'arabiyya kathiiran / anaa atakallamu al-'arabiyya qaliilan

I'm American ___

انا امريكي
anaa amariikiy

Do you speak English? ___

هل تتكلم الانكليزية؟
hal tatakallamu al-inkiliiziyah?

Is there anyone who ___
speaks...?

هل يوجد من يتكلم ال...؟
hal yuujad man yatakallmu al...?

I beg your pardon / what?___

عفوا ماذا قلت/ماذا؟
'afwan maadhaa qulta / maadhaa?

I don't understand ___

لم افهم
lam afham

Do you understand me? ___

هل تفهمني؟
hal tafhamunii?

Could you repeat that, ___
please?

هل يمكن ان تعيد ما قلت، من فضلك؟
hal yumkin an tu'iid maa qulta, min fadlik?

Could you speak more ___
slowly, please?

هل يمكن ان تتكلم ببطء، من فضلك؟
hal yumkin an tatakallama bi-but'in min fadlik?

What does that / that ___
word mean?

ماذا يعني ذلك/ ماذا تعني تلك
الكلمة؟
maadhaa ya'nii dhaalik / maadhaa ta'nii tilka al-kalimah?

It's more or less the ___
same as...

هي تقريبا نفس معنى كلمة...
hiya taqriiban nafsu ma'na kalimat...

Could you write that ___
down for me, please?

هل يمكن ان تكتب لي ذلك من فضلك؟
hal yumkin an taktuba lii dhaalik min fadlik?

Could you spell that for ___
me, please?

هل يمكن ان تتهجى لي ذلك من فضلك؟
hal yumkin an tatahajjaa lii dhaalik min fadlik?

(See 1.8 Telephone alphabets)

Could you point that out ___
in this phrase book, please?

هل يمكن ان تشير الى ذلك في الكتاب،
من فضلك؟
hal yumkin an tushiira ilaa dhaalik fil-kitaab, min fadlik?

Just a minute, I'll look it up ___ دقيقة واحدة، سوف ابحث عن ذلك
daqiiqa wahida, sawfa abhathu 'an dhaalik

I can't find the word / the ___ لا استطيع ان اجد هذه الكلمة/الجملة
sentence
laa astatii'u an ajida haadhihi al-kalima / al-jumla

How do you say that in...? ___ كيف تقول ذلك في اللغة...؟
kayfa taquul dhaalika fii al-lugha...?

How do you pronounce ___ كيف تلفظ ذلك؟
that?
kayfa talfaz dhaalika?

3.2 Introductions

May I introduce myself? ___ إسمح لي ان اقدم نفسي؟
ismah lii an uqaddima nafsii?

My name's... ___ إسمي...
ismii...

I'm... ___ انا...
anaa...

What's your name? ___ ما اسمك؟/ما اسم حضرتك؟
(formal / informal)
maa ismuk? / maa ismu hadratik?

May I introduce...? ___ إسمح لي ان اقدم لك...؟
ismah lii an uqaddima laka...?

This is my wife / husband ___ هذه زوجتي/هذا زوجي
haadhihi zawjatii / haadhaa zawjii

This is my daughter / son ___ هذه ابنتي/هذا ابني
haadhihi ibnatii / haadhaa ibnii

This is my mother / father ___ هذا والدي (ابي)/هذه امي (والدتي)
haadhaa waalidii (abii) / haadhihi ummii (waalidatii)

This is my fiancée / fiancé ___ هذه خطيبتي/هذا خطيبي
haadhihi khatiibatii / haadhaa khatiibii

This is my friend (f/m) ___ هذا صديقي/هذه صديقتي
haadhaa sadiiqii / haadhihi sadiiqatii

How do you do? ___ كيف حالك؟
kayfa haaluk?

Hi, nice to meet you ___ اهلا، مسرور للقائك
(informal)
ahlan, masruur liliqaa'ik

Pleased to meet you ___ أنا سعيد بلقائك
(formal)
anaa sa'iid bi-liqaa'ik

Where are you from? ___ من اي بلد انت؟
min ayyi baladin ant?

I'm American	انا امريكي
	anaa amariikiyy

What city do you live in?	في اي مدينة تسكن؟
	fii ayyati madiinatin taskun?

In...near...	في...قرب...
	fii...qurb...

Have you been here long?	هل جئت منذ وقت طويل؟
	hal ji'ta mundhu waqtin tawiilin?

A few days	بضعة ايام
	bid'at ayyaam.

How long are you staying here?	كم ستقيم (ستبقى) هنا؟
	kam satuqiim (satabqaa) hunaa?

We're probably leaving tomorrow / in two weeks	محتمل ان نغادر غدا/بعد اسبوعين
	muhtamal an nughadir ghadan / ba'da usbuu'ayn

Where are you (m/f) staying?	اين تقيم/تقيمين؟
	ayna tuqiim / tuqiimiin?

I'm staying in a hotel / an apartment	اقيم في فندق/شقة
	uqiimu fii fundiq / shaqqa

At a campsite	في مخيم
	fii mukhayyam

I'm staying with friends / relatives	اقيم مع اصدقاء/أقارب
	uqiimu ma'a asdiqaa' / aqaarib

Are you here on your own / with your family?	هل انت هنا لوحدك/مع عائلتك؟
	hal anta huna liwahdik / ma'a 'aa'ilatik?

I'm on my own	انا لوحدي
	anaa liwahdii

I'm with my partner / wife / husband	انا مع رفيقي (قريني)/زوجتي/زوجي
	anaa ma'a rafiiqii (qariinii) / zawjatii / zawjii

- with my family	مع عائلتي
	ma'a 'aa'ilatii

- with relatives	مع اقاربي
	ma'a aqaaribii

- with a friend / friends	مع صديق/اصدقاء
	ma'a sadiiq / asdiqaa'

Are you married? (m/f)	هل انت متزوج/متزوجة؟
	hal anta mutazawwij / anti mutazawwija?

Are you engaged? _____	هل انت مخطوبة؟ hal anti makhtuuba?
Do you have a steady _____ boyfriend / girlfriend?	هل لك صديق ثابت/صديقة ثابتة؟ hal laki sadiiq thaabit/sadiika thaabita?
That's none of your _____ business	هذا الامر لا يخصلك haadhaa al-amr laa yakhusuk
I'm married (m/f) _____	انا متزوج/متزوجة anaa mutazawwij / mutazawwija
I'm single (m) _____	انا أعزب anaa a'zab
I'm not married (m/f) _____	انا لست متزوجا/متزوجة anaa lastu mutazawwij / mutazawwija
I'm separated (m/f) _____	انا منفصل/انا منفصلة anaa munfasil / munfasila
I'm divorced (m/f) _____	انا مطلق/مطلقة anaa mutallaq / mutallaqa
I'm a widow / widower _____	انا ارملة/ارمل anaa armala / armal
I live alone / with someone __	انا اسكن لوحدي/مع شخص ما anaa askun liwahdii / ma'a shakhsin maa
Do you have any children / __ grandchildren?	هل لديك اي اطفال/احفاد؟ hal ladayka ayya atfaal / ahfaad?
How old are you? _____	كم عمرك؟ kam 'umruk?
How old is she / he? _____	كم عمرها/عمره؟ kam 'umruhaa / 'umruhu?
I'm...(years old) _____	عمري... 'umrii...
She's / he's...(years old) __	عمرها/عمره... 'umruhaa / 'umruhu...
What do you do for a _____ living?	ماذا تعمل؟ maadhaa ta'mal?
I work in an office _____	اعمل في مكتب (دائرة) a'mal fii maktab (daa'ira)
I'm a student (m/f) _____	انا طالب/طالبة anaa taalib / taaliba
I'm unemployed (m/f) _____	لا اعمل (عاطل/عاطلة عن العمل) laa a'mal ('aatil/'aatila 'an al-'amal)

I'm retired _____	انا متقاعد
	anaa mutaqaa'id
I'm on a disability pension __	انا اتقاضى منحة الإعاقة
	anaa ataqaadaa minhat al-i'aqa
I'm a housewife _____	انا ربة بيت
	anaa rabbatu bayt
Do you like your job? _____	هل تحب عملك؟
	hal tuhibbu 'amalak?
Most of the time _____	اكثر الاوقات
	akthar al-awqaat
Mostly I do, but I prefer_____ vacations	نعم غالبا، لكن افضل الإجازات
	na'am ghaaliban, laakin ufadil al-'ijaazaat

3.3 Starting / ending a conversation

Could I ask you something? __ (formal / informal)	هل يمكن ان اسالك شيئا/لدي سؤال؟
	hal yumkin an as'alaka shay'an / ladayya su'aal?
Excuse me (formal / _____ informal)	اعذرني/ارجو المعذرة
	u'dhrnii / arjuu al-ma'dhira
Could you help me, please?__	هل تستطيع ان تساعدني من فضلك؟
	hal tastatii'u an tusaa'idanii min fadlik?
Yes, what's the problem? ____	نعم، ما المشكلة؟
	na'am, maa l-mushkila?
What can I do for you? _____	كيف يمكن ان اساعدك؟
	kayfa yumkin an usaa'idaka?
Sorry, I don't have time now _	عفوا، ليس لدي وقت الان
	'afwan, laysa ladayya waqtun al'aan
Do you have a light? _____	هل لديك قداحة؟
	hal ladayka qaddaaha?
May I join you? _____	هل يمكن ان انضم إليكم؟
	hal yumkin an andamma ilaykum?
Could you take a picture ____ of me / us?	هل يمكن ان تأخذ لي/لنا صورة؟
	hal yumkin an ta'khudha lii /lanaa suura?
Leave me alone! (formal /____ informal)	ارجو ان تتركني لحالي/اتركني لوحدي
	arjuuk an tatrukanii lihaalii / utruknii liwahdii!
Get lost! (formal / informal) __	انصرف عني/ارجوك أن تذهب من هنا
	insarif 'annii / arjuuka an tadhhaba min hunaa!

| Go away or I'll scream _____ | ابعد عني والا سأصرخ |
| | ib'id 'annii wa illaa sa-aṣrukh |

3.4 Congratulations and condolences

| Happy birthday / many happy returns / happy name day _____ | عيد ميلاد سعيد/عمر طويل/يوم سعيد |
| | 'iid miilaad sa'iid / 'umr ṭawiil / yawm sa'iid |

| Please accept my _____ condolences | تعازينا |
| | ta'aaziina |

| My deepest sympathy _____ | مع أخلص مشاعرنا |
| | ma'a akhlaṣ mashaa'irinaa |

3.5 A chat about the weather

See also 1.5 The weather

| It's so hot / cold today! _____ | اليوم الطقس حار / بارد جدا |
| | al-yawm aṭ-ṭaqs ḥaar / baarid jiddan |

| Isn't it a lovely day? _____ | أليس اليوم جميلا؟ |
| | alaysa al-yawm jamiil? |

| It's so windy / what a storm! _____ | هواء شديد / يالها من عاصفة |
| | hawaa'un shadiid / ya lahaa min 'aaṣifa! |

| All that rain / snow! _____ | كل هذا المطر / الثلج! |
| | kullu haadhaa al-maṭar / ath-thalj! |

| It's so foggy! _____ | ضباب شديد! |
| | ḍabaab shadiid! |

| Has the weather been like this for long? _____ | هل كان الطقس هكذا منذ وقت طويل؟ |
| | hal kaana ṭ-ṭaqsu haakadhaa mundhu waqt ṭawiil? |

| Is it always this hot / cold here? _____ | الطقس هنا دائما حار / بارد؟ |
| | aṭ-ṭaqsu hunaa daa'iman ḥaar / baarid? |

| Is it always this dry / humid here? _____ | الطقس هنا دائما جاف / رطب؟ |
| | aṭ-ṭaqsu hunaa daa'iman jaaf / raṭib? |

3.6 Hobbies

| Do you have any hobbies? _____ | هل لديك اية هوايات؟ |
| | hal ladyka ayyat hiwaayaat? |

| I like knitting / reading / photography _____ | انا احب الحياكة / القرائة / التصوير |
| | anaa uḥibbu al-ḥiyaaka / al-qiraa'a / at-taṣwiir |

| I enjoy listening to music _____ | انا احب الإستماع الى الموسيقى |
| | anaa uḥibbu al-istimaa'a ilaa al-muusiiqaa |

I play the guitar / the piano	انا اعزف على الكيتار / البيانو anaa a'zifu 'alaa al-kitaar / al-biyaanu
I like the cinema	احب السينما uhibbu as-siinamaa
I like traveling / playing sports / going fishing/ going for a walk	احب السفر /الرياضة/الصيد/التمشي uhibbu as-safar / ar-riyada / as-sayd / al-tamashyi

3.7 Being the host(ess)

See also 4 Eating out

Can I offer you a drink? (formal / informal)	هل تريد مشروبا ؟ hal triidu mashruban?
What would you like to drink? (formal / informal)	مذا تحب ان تشرب؟ maadhaa tuhib an tashrab?
Something non-alcoholic, please	أي شيء غير الكحول من فضلك ayya shay'in ghayr al-kuhuul min fadlik
Would you like a cigarette?	هل تريد سيجارة ؟ hal turiid siijaara?
I don't smoke	انا لا ادخن anaa laa udakhin

3.8 Invitations

Are you doing anything tonight?	هل انت مشغول الليلة ؟ hal anta mashghuul al-layla?
Do you have any plans for today / this afternoon / tonight?	هل لديك برنامج لهذا اليوم/اليوم بعد الظهر /الليلة؟ hal ladyaka barnaamaj lihaadhaa al-yawm / al-yawm ba'da z-zuhr / al-layla?
Would you like to go out with me?	هل تحب ان نخرج سوية ؟ hal tuhib an nakhruja sawiyyatan?
Would you like to go dancing with me?	هل تحب ان نذهب إلى الرقص؟ hal tuhib an nadhhaba ilaa r-raqsi?
Would you like to have lunch / dinner with me?	هل تحب ان تأتي معي للغداء /للعشاء؟ hal tuhib an ta'tiya ma'ii lilghadaa' / lil'ashaa'?
Would you like to come to the beach with me?	هل تحب ان تأتي معي إلى الشاطئ؟ hal tuhib an ta'tiya ma'ii ilaa sh-shaati'?

Conversation

Would you like to come ____ into town with us?	هل تحب ان تاتي معنا الى المدينة؟ hal tuhib an ta'tiya ma'anaa ilaa l-madiina?
Would you like to come and _ see some friends with us?	هل تحب ان تأتي معنا لزيارة بعض الاصدقاء؟ hal tuhib an ta'tiya ma'anaa liziyaarat ba'd l-asdiqaa'?
Shall we dance? _____	هل تحب أن نرقص؟ hal tuhib an narqusa?
- sit at the bar? _____	هل نجلس في البار؟ hal najlis fii l-baar?
- get something to drink? ___	هل تريد مشروبا ما؟ hal turiid mashruuban maa?
Shall we go for a walk / ____ drive?	هل تريد اب نتمشى (نتجول بالسيارة)؟ hal turiid an natamashaa (natajawwal bi s-sayyaara)?
Yes, all right _____	نعم، هذا جيد na'm, haadhaa jayyid
Good idea _____	فكرة جيدة fikra jayyida
No thank you _____	لا شكرا laa shukran
Maybe later _____	ربما فيما بعد rubbamaa fiimaa ba'd
I don't feel like it _____	لا اشعر برغبة في laa ash'ur biraghbatin fii
I don't have time _____	ليس لدي وقت laysa ladyya waqt
I already have a date _____	انا لدي موعد anaa ladayya maw'id
I'm not very good at dancing / volleyball / swimming	انا لا أجيد الرقص/كرة الطائرة/السباحة anaa laa ujiidu ar-raqs / al-kurat at-taa'ira / as-sibaaha

3.9 Paying a compliment

You look great! (f/m) _____	كم أنت جميلة/أنت وسيم kam anti jamiila / anta wasiim
I like your car! _____	سيارتك تعجبني! sayyaaratuka tu'jibunii!
I like your ski outfit! _____	تعجبني لباس التزلج لديك tu'jibunii libaasu t-tazalluji ladayka!

You are very nice (m/f) _____ أنت لطيف/أنت لطيفة
anta laṭiif / anti laṭiifa

What a good boy / girl! _____ حقا إنه ولد ممتاز/بنت ممتازة
ḥaqqan innahu walad mumtaaz / bint
mumtaaza!

You're a good dancer (m/f) ___ أنت راقص جيد/أنت راقصة جيدة
anta raaqiṣ jayyid / anti raaqiṣa jayyida

You're a very good cook _____ أنت طباخ جيد جدا
anta ṭabbaakh jayyid jiddan

You're a good soccer player__ أنت لاعب كرة قدم ماهر
antaa laa'ib kurat qadam maahir

3.10 Intimate comments / questions

I like being with you _____ احب ان اكون معك
uḥibbu an akuuna ma'ak

I've missed you so much ___ انا مشتاق اليك
anaa mushtaaqun ilayk

I dreamt about you (m/f) _____ حلمت بك
ḥalimtu bika / biki

I think about you all day _____ انا افكر فيك طول اليوم
anaa ufakkiru fiiki ṭuul al-yawm

I've been thinking about _____ كنت افكر فيك طول اليوم
you all day kuntu ufakkiru fiiki ṭuul al-yawm

You have such a sweet _____ لديك ابتسامة جميلة
smile ladayki ibtisaama jamiila

You have such beautiful _____ عيونك جميلة
eyes 'uyuunuki jamiila

I'm fond of you (m/f) _____ انا مغرم/مغرمة بك
anaa mughram / mughrama bik

I love you _____ انا احب
anaa uḥibbuk

I love you too _____ انا احبك ايضا
anaa uḥibbuk aydan

I'm in love with you _____ انا وقعت في حبك
anaa waqa'tu fii ḥubbik

I'm in love with you too ____ انا ايضا وقعت في حبك
anaa aydan waq'atu fii ḥubbik

I don't feel as strongly _____ مشاعري تجاهك ليست قوية
about you mashaa'irii tujaahak laysat
qawiyyatan

| I already have a girlfriend / boyfriend | انا لدي صديقة/صديق |
| | anaa ladyya <u>s</u>adiiqa / <u>s</u>adiiq |

I'm not ready for that _____ لست مستعدا لذلك
lastu musta'iddan li<u>dh</u>aalik

I don't want to rush into it ___ لا اريد ان اكون مستعجلا في ذلك
laa uriidu an akuuna musta'jilan fii
<u>dh</u>aalik

Take your hands off me _____ إرفع يدك عني
irfa' yadaka 'annii

Okay, no problem _____ طيب ليست هناك مشكلة
<u>t</u>ayyib laysat hunaaka mu<u>sh</u>kila

Will you spend the night ____ هل تقضين الليلة معي؟
with me? hal taqddiina al-layla ma'ii?

I'd like to go to bed with ____ احب أن انام معك
you u<u>h</u>ibbu an anaama ma'aki

Only if we use a condom ____ فقط اذا استخدمنا الغلاف المطاطي
(الكبوت)
faqat i<u>dh</u>aa ista<u>kh</u>damnaa al-<u>gh</u>ilaaf al-
matta<u>t</u>ii (al-kabuut)

We have to be careful _____ يجب ان نكون حذرين من الايدز
about AIDS yajib an nakuuna <u>h</u>a<u>dh</u>iriin mina al-
aydiz

That's what they all say ____ هذا ما يقوله الجميع
haa<u>dh</u>aa maa yaquluhu al-jamii'

We shouldn't take any risks __ يجب ان لا نجازف
yajibu an laa nujaazif

Do you have a condom? ____ هل لديك الغلاف المطاطي (الكبوت)؟
hal ladayka al-<u>gh</u>ilaaf al-matta<u>t</u>ii?

No? Then the answer's no ___ لا؟ اذن الجواب لا
laa? i<u>dh</u>an al-jawaab laa

3.11 Arrangements

When will I see you again? ___ متى سأراك مرة اخرى؟
mataa sa-araaka marratan u<u>kh</u>raa?

Are you free over the _____ هل لديك وقت خلال عطلة نهاية الاسبوع؟
weekend? hal ladayk waqtun <u>kh</u>ilaal 'u<u>t</u>lat
nihaayat al-usbuu'?

What's the plan, then? _____ ما الخطة (البرنامج) اذن؟
maa al-<u>kh</u>u<u>tt</u>a (al-barnaamaj) i<u>dh</u>an?

Where shall we meet? _____ اين سنلتقي؟
ayna sanaltaqii?

Will you pick me / us up? _____	هل ستحملني/هل ستصحبني معك في السيارة؟
	hal satahmilunii / hal satas-habunii ma'aka fii s-sayyaara?
Shall I pick you up? _____	هل تريدني ان اصحبك معي في السيارة؟
	hal turiidunii an as-habaka ma'ii fii as-sayyaara?
I have to be home by... _____	يجب ان اكون في البيت الساعة...
	yajibu an akuuna fii al-bayt as-saa'a...
I don't want to see you anymore _____	لا اريد ان اراك مرة اخرى ابدا
	laa uriidu an araaka marratan ukhraa abadan

3.12 Saying goodbye

Can I take you home? _____	هل تريد ان اصطحبك إلى البيت؟
	hal turiidu an astahibaka ilaa al-bayt?
Can I write / call you? _____	هل يمكن ان اراسلك/اتصل بك؟
	hal yumkin an uraasilak / attasil bik?
Will you write to me / call me? _____	هل ستراسلني/تتصل بي؟
	hal sa-turaasilunii / tattasil bii?
Can I have your address / phone number? _____	هل يمكن ان تعطيني عنوانك/رقم هاتفك؟
	hal yumkin an tu'tiyanii 'unwaanak / raqam haatifik?
Thanks for everything _____	شكرا على كل شيئ
	shukran 'alaa kulli shay'
It was a lot of fun _____	كانت ممتعة
	kaanat mumti'a
Say hello to... _____	بلغ تحياتي لـ...
	balligh tahiyyaatii li...
All the best _____	اتمنى لك كل الخير
	atamanna laka kulla alkhayr
Good luck _____	حظا سعيدا
	hazzan sa'iidan
When will you be back? _____	متى ستعود؟
	mataa sata'uud?
I'll be waiting for you _____	سوف اكون بانتظارك
	sawfa akuun bintizaarik
I'd like to see you again _____	احب ان اراك مرة اخرى
	uhibbu an araaka marratan ukhraa

Conversation

I hope we meet again soon ___ أتمنى ان نلتقي مرة اخرى قريبا
atamannaa an naltaqii marratan
u<u>kh</u>raa qariiban

Here's our address. If ___ هذا عنواننا إذا صادف أن زرت
you're ever in the United أمريكا...
States...
haa<u>dh</u>aa 'unwaanunaa, i<u>dh</u>aa <u>s</u>aadafa
an zurta amariika...

You'd be more than ___ نرحب بك دائما
welcome nura<u>hh</u>ibu bika daa'iman

Eating out

4 Eating out

Eating establishments

Mealtimes

The Middle East is an ecologically diverse area, so it is important to remember that as such most societies conduct their lives in ways that reflect their environment as well as their specific social and cultural heritage. Nevertheless, eating is one of the common cultural practices in most countries of the Middle East where people usually not only eat but celebrate life through eating. Each meal is a family occasion and guests (including strangers) are warmly invited to share whatever is prepared. Like other countries, the three main meals are:

1. **fatour as-sabaah** (breakfast), eaten sometime between 7.30 and 9.00 a.m. It generally consists of bread, eggs, olives and tea. In the Arab countries of North Africa, croissant, toast (with butter, honey and jam) and milk coffee are also common.
2. **ghadaa'** (lunch), traditionally eaten at home between 12.00 and 1.30 p.m., includes pickles, salads, breads / rice and a hot (meat) dish.
3. **ashaa'** (dinner), at around 7.00 or 8.00 p.m., is a light meal, often including salad, soup and sometimes leftovers from the main lunch.

In restaurants

Most restaurants have a cover charge which includes bread, pickled vegetables, olives and dips. In most countries, no specific service charge is required.

4.1 On arrival

I'd like to reserve a table for seven o'clock, please	أريد ان احجز طاولة الساعة السابعة من فضلك uriidu an ahjiza taawila assaa'a assaabi'ah min fadlik
A table for two, please	طاولة لشخصين/لنفرين من فضلك taawila li <u>shakh</u>sayn (li nafarayn) min fadlik

هل لديك حجز؟ hal ladayka hajz?	Do you have a reservation?
الاسم من فضلك؟ al-ism min fadlik?	What name, please?
تفضل من هنا tafadal min hunaa	This way, please
هذه الطاولة محجوزة haadhihi at taawila mahjuuza	This table is reserved
سوف تتوفر طاولة بعد خمسة عشرة دقيقة sawfa tatawaffar taawila ba'da khamsat 'ashara daqiiqa	We'll have a table free in fifteen minutes
لو سمحت ممكن ان تنتظر؟ law samaht mumkin an tantazir?	Would you mind waiting?

We've reserved _____	لم نحجز lam nahjiz
Is the restaurant open yet? __	هل مازال المطعم مفتوحا ؟ hal mazaala al-mat'am maftuuhan?
What time does the _____ restaurant open? / What time does the restaurant close?	متى يفتح المطعم؟/متى يغلق المطعم؟ mataa yaftah al-mat'am? / mataa yughliq al-mat'am?
Can we wait for a table? _____	هل يمكن ان ننتظر لحين توفر طاولة ؟ hal yumkin an nantazir lihiin tawaffur taawila?
Do we have to wait long? ___	هل سننتظر طويلا ؟ hal sa-nantazir tawiilan?
Is this seat taken? _____	هل هذا المقعد محجوز ؟ hal haadhaa al-maq'ad mahjuuz?
Could we sit here / there? ___	هل يمكن ان نجلس هنا/هناك ؟ hal yumkin an najlisa hunaa / hunaak?
Can we sit by the window? __	هل يمكن ان نجلس بجانب الشباك ؟ hal yumkin an najlisa bijaanib ash-shubbaak?
Are there any tables _____ outside?	هل توجد طاولات في الخارج ؟ hal tuujad taawilaat fil-khaarij?
Do you have another chair ___ for us?	هل لديك كرسي اخر ؟ hal ladayka kursiy aakhar?
Do you have a highchair? ___	هل لديك كرسي أطفال ؟ hal ladayka kursiy atfaal?
Is there a socket for this _____ bottle-warmer?	هل يوجد مقبس لمسخن القوارير هذا ؟ hal yuujad miqbas li-musakhin al-qawaariir haadha?
Could you warm up this _____ bottle / jar for me?	هل يمكن ان تسخن هذه القنينة ؟ hal yumkin an tusakhina haadhihi al-qannina?
Not too hot, please _____	ليس حارا جدا من فضلك laysa haaran jiddan min fadlik
Is there somewhere I can ___ change the baby's diaper?	اين يمكن ان اغير حفاظ الطفل ؟ ayna yumkin an ughayira haffaaz at-tifl?
Where are the restrooms? ___	اين توجد المرافق الصحية ؟ ayna tuujad al-maraafiq al-sihiya?

4

Eating out

Eating out

4.2 Ordering

Waiter / Waitress! _____	أيها النادل/النادلة
	ayyuhaa an-naadil / an-naadila
Madam! _____	سيدتي
	sayidatii
Sir _____	سيدي
	sayidii
We'd like something to _____ eat / drink	نريد شيئا نأكل/نشرب
	nuriid shai'an na'kul / nashrab
Could I have a quick meal? __	هل يمكن ان احصل على وجبة سريعة
	hal yumkin an ahsula 'alaa wajba sarii'a?
We don't have much time ___	ليس لدينا الكثير من الوقت
	laysa ladainaa al-kathiir mina al-waqt
We'd like to have a drink ___ first	اولا نريد ان نشرب
	awwalan nuriidu an nashraba
Could we see the menu / _____ wine list, please?	هل يمكن ان نطلع على قائمة الماكولات/ المشروبات من فضلك؟
	hal yumkin an nattali'a 'alaa qaa'imat al-ma'kuulaat / al-mashruubaat min fadlik?
Do you have a menu in _____ English?	هل لديكم قائمة مأكولات باللغة الإنكليزية؟
	hal ladayka qaa'imat ma'kuulaat bil-lugha al-inkliziya?
Do you have a dish of the ___ day / a tourist menu?	هل لديكم طبق اليوم/قائمة طعام السائح؟
	hal ladaykum tabaq al-yawm / qaa'imat ta'aam as-saa'ih?
We haven't made a choice __ yet	لم نقرر بعد
	lam nuqarrir ba'du
What do you recommend? __	بماذا تنصح؟
	bi-maadhaa tansah?
What are the local _____ specialities?	ما هي الأطباق المحلية لديكم؟
	maa hiya al-atbaaq al-mahalliya ladaykum?
I like strawberries / olives ___	اريد فراولة/زيتون
	uriidu faraawla / zaytuun
I don't like meat / fish _____	لا أحب اللحم/السمك
	laa uhibbu al-lahma / as-samaka
What's this? _____	ما هذا؟
	maa haadhaa?

Does it have...in it? _____ هل يوجد ...فيه؟
hal yuujad ...fiihi?

Is it stuffed with...? _____ هل هذا محشو بـ...؟
hal haadhaa mahshuu bi...?

What does it taste like? _____ ما طعمه؟
maa ta'muhu?

Is this a hot or a cold dish? ___ هل هذا طبق حار ام بارد؟
hal haadhaa tabaq haar am baarid?

Is this sweet? _____ هل هذا حلو؟
hal haadhaa hulw?

Is this hot (spicy)? _____ هل هذا حار (فيه فلفل حار)؟
hal haadhaa haar (fiihi fulful haar)?

Do you have anything else, ___ هل لديكم اي شيء اخر؟
by any chance? hal ladaykum ay shay' aakhar?

I'm on a salt-free diet _____ انا اريد طعاما خاليا من الملح
anaa uriid ta'aaman khaaliyan min al-milh

I can't eat pork _____ انا لا اكل لحم الخنزير
anaa laa aakulu lahma l-khanziir

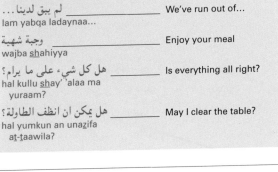

ماذا تطلب؟ _____ What would you like?
maadhaa tatlub?

هل قررتم؟ _____ Have you decided?
hal qarratum?

هل ترغبون بالشراب اولا؟ _____ Would you like a drink first?
hal targhabuun bish-sharaab awwalan?

ماذا تحبون أن تشربوا اولا؟ _____ What would you like to drink?
maadhaa tuhibbuun an tashrabuu awwalan?

لم يبق لدينا... _____ We've run out of...
lam yabqa ladaynaa...

وجبة شهية _____ Enjoy your meal
wajba shahiyya

هل كل شيء على ما يرام؟ _____ Is everything all right?
hal kullu shay' 'alaa ma yuraam?

هل يمكن ان انظف الطاولة؟ _____ May I clear the table?
hal yumkun an unazifa at-taawila?

4 Eating out

I can't have sugar _____	انا لا استطيع ان آخذ السكر	anaa laa asstatii'u an aakhudha as-sukkar.
I'm on a fat-free diet _____	اريد طعاما خاليا من الدسم	uriid ta'aaman khaaliyan min ad-dassim
I can't have spicy food _____	لا استطيع ان اتناول طعاما فيه فلفل حار	laa asstatii'u an atanaawala ta'aaman fiihi fulful haar
We'll have what those people are having	نريد نفس طبق اولئك الناس	nuriid nafs tabaq 'ulaa'ika an-naas
I'd like... _____	ارغب في...	arghabu fii...
We're not having a rice dish _	ليس لدينا طبق الارز	laysa ladaynaa tabaq al-aruz
Could I have some more bread, please?	هل يمكن ان احصل على المزيد من الخبز من فضلك	hal yumkin an ahsula 'alaa al-maziid mina al-khubz, min fadlik
Could I have another bottle of water / wine, please?	هل يمكن ان احصل على قنينة/نبيذ اخرى من فضلك	hal yumkin an ahsula 'alaa qinninat nabiidh / ukhraa, min fadlik
Could I have another portion of..., please?	هل يمكن ان احصل على قطعة اخرى من ...من فضلك	hal yumkin an ahsula 'alaa qit'a ukhraa min..., min fadlik
Could I have the salt and pepper, please?	هل يمكن ان احصل على ملح وفلفل من فضلك	hal yumkin an ahsula 'alaa milh wa fulful, min fadlik
Could I have a napkin, please?	هل يمكن ان احصل على منديل من فضلك	hal yumkin an ahsula 'alaa mindiil, min fadlik
Could I have a teaspoon, please?	هل يمكن ان احصل على ملعقة من فضلك	hal yumkin an ahsula 'alaa mil'aqa, min fadlik
Could I have an ashtray, please?	هل يمكن ان احصل على...من فضلك	hal yumkin an ahsula 'alaa..., min fadlik
Could I have some matches, please?	هل يمكن ان احصل على كبريت من فضلك	hal yumkin an ahsula 'alaa kibriit, min fadlik

Could I have some _____ toothpicks, please?	هل يمكن ان احصل على اعواد تنظيف الاسنان من فضلك
	hal yumkin an ahsul 'alaa a'waad tanziif al-asnaan, min fadlik
Could I have a glass of _____ water, please?	هل يمكن ان احصل على كأس ماء من فضلك
	hal yumkin an ahsulu 'alaa ka's maa', min fadlik
Could I have a straw, _____ please?	هل يمكن ان احصل على سيفونة (مصاصة للشرب) من فضلك
	hal yumkin an ahsula 'alaa siifuna (massaasa lish-shuurb), min fadlik
Enjoy your meal! _____	وجبة شهية
	wajba shahiyya!
You too! _____	وانت كذلك
	wa anta kadhaalik!
Cheers! _____	صحتين
	sahtiin!
The next round's on me _____	المرة القادمة على حسابي أنا
	al-marra al-qaadima 'alaa hisaabii anaa
Could we have a doggy _____ bag, please?	لو سمحت هل يمكن ان نحصل على كيس للكلب؟
	law samaht, hal yumkin an nahsula 'alaa kiis li-lkalb?

4.3 The bill

See also 8.2 Settling the bill

How much is this dish? _____	كم سعر هذا الطبق؟
	kam si'ru haadhaa t-tabaq?
Could I have the bill, please? _____	الفاتورة من فضلك؟
	al-faatuura min fadlik?
All together _____	جميعا
	jamii'an
Everyone pays separately _____	كل واحد يدفع عن نفسه
	kul waahid yadfa' 'an nafsihi
Could we have the menu _____ again, please?	هل يمكن ان نحصل على القائمة مرة اخرى، من فضلك؟
	hal yumkin an nahsala 'alaa al-qaa'ima marratan ukhraa, min fadlik?
The...is not on the bill _____	الـ...ليس في الفاتورة
	Al...laysa fii l-faatuura

4

Eating out

It's taking a very long time ___	لقد تأخر كثيرا laqad ta'akhara kathiiran
We've been here an hour already ___	نحن هنا منذ ساعة nahnu hunaa mundhu sa'aa
This must be a mistake _____	هذا خطأ بالتأكيد haadhaa khata' bit-ta'kiid
This is not what I ordered ___	ليس هذا ما طلبت laysa haadhaa maa talabtu
I ordered... _____	انا طلبت... anaa talabtu...
There's a dish missing _____	هناك طبق مفقود hunnaka tabaq mafquud
This is broken / not clean ___	هذا مكسور/وسخ haadhaa maksuur / wasikh
The food's cold _____	الطعام بارد at-ta'aamu baarid
The food's not fresh _____	الطعام ليس طازجا at-ta'aamu laysa tazajan
The food's too salty / sweet / spicy _____	الطعام ملح/حلو/حار جدا at-ta'aamu maalih / huluw / haar jiddan
The meat's too rare _____	اللحم ليس مطهو جيدا al-lahmu laysa mathuw jayyidan
The meat's overdone _____	اللحم مطبوخ اكثر من اللازم al-lahmu matbuukh akthar min al-laazim
The meat's tough _____	اللحم ليس طريا al-lahmu laysa tariyyan
The meat is off / has gone bad ___	اللحم فاسد/ردي ء al-lahmu faasid / radii'
Could I have something else instead of this? ___	هل يمكن أن أحصل على شيء غير هذا ؟ hal yumkin an ahsula 'alaa shay' ghayr haadhaa?
The bill / this amount is not right ___	الفاتورة/هذا المبلغ ليس صحيحا al-faatuura / haadhaa al-mablagh laysa sahiihan
We didn't have this _____	لم نأكل هذا lam na'kul haadhaa

There's no toilet paper in ___ the restroom	لا يوجد ورق كلينكس (اوراق تواليت) في المرافق الصحية laa yuujad waraq kliiniks (awraaq twaaliit) fii al-maraafiq as-sihhiyya
Will you call the manager, ___ please?	هل لك أن تنادي المدير من فضلك hal laka an tunaadi al-mudiir min fadlik?

4.5 Paying a compliment

That was a wonderful meal ___	كانت وجبة رائعة kaanat wajba raa'i'a
The food was excellent ___	كان الطعام ممتازا kaana at-ta'aamu mumtaazan
The...in particular was delicious ___	بالخصوص كان الـ...لذيذا bil-khussuus kaana al-...ladhiidhan

4.6 The menu

مقبلات muqabbilaat starter / hors d'oeuvres	جبن jubn (jibn) cheese	سمك samak fish
لعبة lu'ba game	فواكه fawaakih fruit	بيزا piizaa pizza
لحم lahm meat	بوظة buuza ice cream	المفتحات al-mufattihaat first course
طبق غير اساسي / خضروات tabaq ghayr assaasi / khudrawaat side dishes / vegetables	سلطة salata salad	الوجبة الرئيسية al-wajba ar-ra'isiyya main course
	آداء القيمة المضافة adaa' al-qiima al-mudaafa VAT	أجرة الخدمة ujrat al-khidma service charge
أجرة ujra cover charge	شوربة shurba soup	طبق خاص tabak khaas specialities
شراب sharaab liqueur (after dinner)	خبز khubz bread	وجبات خفيفة wajabaat khafiifa snacks
كعك / حلويات ka'k / halawiyyaat cakes / desserts	معكرونة ma'karuuna pasta	خضروات khudrawaat vegetables

55

juice _____	عصير 'aṣiir
rice _____	أرز aruz
orange _____	برتقال burtuqaal
chicken _____	دجاج dajaaj
strawberry _____	فراولة faraawla
fruit _____	فواكه fawaakih
pepper _____	فلفل fulful
spicy / hot _____	حار ḥaar
sweets / cakes _____	حلويات ḥalawiyyaat
cheese _____	جبن jubn
cakes _____	كعك k'ak
bread _____	خبز khubz
vegetables _____	خضروات khudrawaat
meat _____	لحم laḥm
pasta _____	معكرونة ma'karuuna
water _____	ماء maa'
banana _____	موز mawz
pickled vegetables __	مخلل mikhallil
salt _____	ملح milḥ
first course _____	مقبلات muqabbilaat
pizza _____	بيزا piizaa
coffee _____	قهوة qahwa
fish _____	سمك samak
tea _____	شاي shaay
apples _____	تفاح tuffaaḥ
main dish _____	وجبة رئيسية wajba ra'isiyya
olives _____	زيتون zaytuun

5

On the road

5 On the road

5.1 Asking for directions

Excuse me, could I ask _____ you something?	لو سمحت هل يمكن أن أسألك سؤالا ؟ law samahta, hal yumkin an as'alaka su'aalan?
I've lost my way _____	لقد ظللت طريقي laqad zalaltu tariiqii
Is there a...around here? ____	هل يوجد...هنا ؟ hal yuujad...hunaa?
Is this the way to...? _____	هل هذا هو الطريق إلى...؟ hal haadhaa huwa at-tariiqu ilaa..?
Could you tell me how _____ to get to...?	هل تدلني على...؟ hal tadullanii 'alaa...?
What's the quickest way _____ to...?	ما هو أسرع طريق إلى...؟ maa huwa asra' tariiq ilaa...?
How many kilometers is _____ it to...?	كم كيلو متر (المسافة) إلى...؟ kam killumitr (al-massafa) ilaa...?
Could you point it out on _____ the map?	هل تبين لي ذلك على الخارطة؟ hal tubayyin lii dhaalika 'alaa al-khaarita?

لا أعرف، لا أعرف طريقي هنا _____ laa a'rif, laa a'rif tariiqii hunaa	I don't know, I don't know my way around here
أنت ذاهب في الطريق الخطأ _____ anta dhaahib fii t-tariq al-khata'	You're going the wrong way
يجب أن ترجع إلى... yajib an tarji'a ilaa...	You have to go back to...
بعد ذلك إتبع العلامات _____ ba'da dhaalika ittabi 'al-'alaamaat	From there on just follow the signs
عندما تصل إلى هناك إسأل مرة أخرى 'indamaa tasil ilaa hunaak is'al marratan ukhraa	When you get there, ask again

سر إلى الأمام sir 'ila l-'amaam go straight ahead	الطريق/الشارع at-tariiq / ash-shaari' the road / street	النهر an-nahr the river
إنعطف يسارا in'atif yas'aran turn left	الإشارة الضوئية al-ishaara ad-daw'iyya the traffic light	المعبر al-ma'bar the overpass

الجسر	النفق	إنعطف يميناً
al-jisr	an-nafaq	in'atif yamiinan
the bridge	the tunnel	turn right

ممر العبور	علامة الخروج	أعبر
mamarr al-'ubuur	'alaamat al-khuruuj	u'bur
the grade crossing	the "yield" sign	cross

العلامات تشير إلى	البناية	إتبع
al-al'aamaat tushiir ilaa	al-binaaya	ittabi'
the signs pointing to	the building	follow

السهم	عند الزاوية	التقاطع
as-sahm	'inda z-zaawiya	at-taqaat'u
the arrow	at the corner	the intersection / crossroads

5.2 Customs

By law you must always carry with you a passport, and if driving, your driving license.

Most visitors require a visa to enter certain countries of the Middle East, and these should be organized prior to travel arrangements as procedures differ from one country to another.

For car and motorbike: valid driving license, vehicle registration document; third-party international insurance document.

Trailer: same registration number plate and registration documents.

جواز السفر من فضلك _____ jawaazu as-safar min fadlik	Your passport, please
البطاقة الخضراء من فضلك _____ al-bitaaqa al-khadraa' min fadlik	Your green card, please
وثائق سيارتك من فضلك _____ wathaa'iq sayyaaratika min fadlik	Your vehicle documents, please
التأشيرة من فضلك _____ at-ta'shiira min fadlik	Your visa, please
إلى أين أنت ذاهب؟ _____ ilaa ayna anta dhaahib?	Where are you going?
كم يوماً ستبقى هنا؟ _____ kam yawman satabqaa hunaa?	How long are you planning to stay?
هل لديك ما تصرح به؟ _____ hal ladayka maa tusarrih bihi?	Do you have anything to declare?
إفتح هذا من فضلك _____ iftah haadhaa min fadlik	Open this, please

Import and export specifications:

Foreign currency	–	no restrictions
Alcohol	–	prohibited in some countries (Saudi Arabia), but allowed under strict regulations in others (Syria)
Tobacco	–	200 cigarettes, 50 cigars, 250g tobacco
Perfume	–	50g perfume, 250ml eau de toilette
Coffee	–	500g
Tea	–	100g

My children are entered _____ on this passport	أطفالي مسجلون في هذا الجواز atfaalii musajjaluun fii haadha l-jawaaz
I'm traveling through _____	أنا مسافر عن طريق anaa musaafir 'an tariiq
I'm going on vacation to... _____	أنا ذاهب في نزهة إلى... anaa dhaahib fii nuzha ilaa...
I'm on a business trip _____	أنا في رحلة عمل anaa fii rihlat 'amal
I don't know how long _____ I'll be staying	لا أعرف كم سأبقى laa a'rif kam sa'abqaa
I'll be staying here for _____ a weekend	سأبقى هنا إلى نهاية الأسبوع sa-abqaa hunaa ilaa nihaayat al-usbuu
I'll be staying here for _____ a few days	سأقيم هنا لبضعة أيام sa-uqiimu hunaa li-bid'at ayyaam
I'll be staying here a week ___	سأبقى هنا أسبوعا sa-'abqaa hunaa usbuu'an
I'll be staying here for _____ two weeks	سأبقى هنا أسبوعين sa-'abqaa hunaa usbuu'ayn
I've got nothing to declare ___	ليس لدي شيء أصرح به laysa ladayya shay' usariih bihi
I have... _____	لدي... ladayya...
- a carton of cigarettes _____	كرتونة سجائر kartuunat sajaa'ir
- a bottle of... _____	قنينة... qanniinat...
- some souvenirs _____	بعض الهدايا ba'd al-hadaayaa
These are personal items ___	هذه أمتعة شخصية haadhihi amti'a shakhsiya
These are not new _____	هذه ليست جديدة haadhihi laysat jadiida

| Here's the receipt | هذا هو الوصل |
| | haadhaa huwa al-wasl |

| This is for private use | هذا للإستخدام الخاص |
| | haadhaa lil-istikhdaam al-khaas |

| How much import duty do I have to pay? | كم يجب أن أدفع رسوم جمركية؟ |
| | kam yajibu an adfa'a rusuum jumrukiyya? |

| May I go now? | هل أستطيع أن أذهب الآن؟ |
| | hal astatii'u an adhhaba al'aan? |

5.3 Luggage

| Porter! | حمال |
| | hammaal |

| Could you take this luggage to...? | هل تستطيع أن تحمل هذه البضائع إلى...؟ |
| | hal tastatii'u an tahmila haadhihi al-badaa'i' ilaa ...? |

| How much do I owe you? | كم أدفع لك؟ |
| | kam adfa' laka? |

| Where can I find a cart? | أين يمكن أن أجد عربة؟ |
| | ayna yumkin an ajida 'araba? |

| Could you store this luggage for me? | هل يمكن أن تخزن لي هذه البضائع؟ |
| | hal yumkin an takhzina lii haadhihi al-badaa'i'? |

| Where are the luggage lockers? | أين خزانة حفظ البضائع؟ |
| | ayna khizaanat hifz al-badaa'i'? |

| I can't get the locker open | هل أستطيع أن أفتح الخزانة |
| | hal astatii'u an aftaha al-khizaana |

| How much is it per item per day? | كم يجب أن أدفع في اليوم مقابل كل قطعة؟ |
| | kam yajib an adfa'a fii al-yawm muqaabil kulli qit'a? |

| This is not my suitcase | هذه ليست حقيبتي |
| | haadhihi laysat haqiibatii |

| There's one item / suitcase missing | هناك حقيبة/كيس مفقود |
| | hunaaka haqiiba / kiis mafquud |

| My suitcase is damaged | حقيبتي تالفة |
| | haqiibatii taalifa |

On the road

5

أنر المصابيح الامامية في النفق
anir al-maṣabiiḥ al-amaamiya
fii al-nafaq
turn on headlights (in the
tunnel)

قف
qif
stop

محطة بنزين
maḥaṭṭat banziin
service station

إحذر
iḥdhar
beware

شاحنات ثقيلة
shaaḥinaat thaqiila
heavy trucks

ممر مغلق
mamarr mughlaq
impassible shoulder

إحذر، صخور متساقطة
iḥdhar, ṣukhuur mutasaaqiṭa
beware, falling rocks

تغيير مسارات
taghyiir masaaraat
change lanes

طريق مغلق
ṭariiq mughlaq
road closed

رواق طواريء
riwaaq ṭawaari'
emergency lane

منعطفات
mun'aṭafaat
curves

تغيير وجهة
taghyiir wijha
detour

موقف إجباري
mawqif ijbaarii
parking disk (compulsory)

أولوية المرور عند نهاية الطريق
awlawiyyat al-muruur 'inda
nihaayat aṭ-ṭariiq
right of way at end of road

ممنوع المرور
mamnuu' al-muruur
no passing

تقاطع
taqqaaṭu'
intersection/crossroads

جزيرة مرور / طريق للمترجلين
ṭariiq lil-mutarajjiliin / jazira
muruur
traffic island / pedestrian walk

لا تعرقل سير الطريق
laa tu'arqil sayra ṭ-ṭariiq
do not obstruct

أشغال على الطريق
ashghaal 'alaa ṭ-ṭariiq
road works

أجرة رسوم الطريق
ujrat rusuum aṭ-ṭariiq
toll payment

موقف سيارات بـأجرة / موقف
محجوز
mawqif sayyaaraat bi'ujra /
mawqif maḥjuuz
paying carpark / parking
reserved for

موقف سيارات مراقب
mawqif sayyaaraat muraaqab
supervised parking

...ممر للعبور
mamarr li-l'ubuur
grade crossing

العدد الأقصى للركاب
al-'ada al-aqṣaa lir-rukkaab
maximum headroom

مدخل
madkhal
driveway

خطر
khatar
danger(ous)

مطر أو ثلج بعد...كيلومتر
matar aw thalj ba'da...
  kiilumitr
rain or ice for...kms

أولوية المرور
awlawiyyat al-muruur
right of way

خفف السرعة
khaffif as-sur'a
slow down

إتجاه واحد
ittijaah waahid
one way

ممنوع الدخول
mamnuu' ad-dukhuul
no entry

مساعدة على الطريق
musaa'ada 'alaa t-tariiq
road assistance (breakdown
  service)

موقف مؤقت
mawqif mu'aqqat
parking for a limited period

طريق متعرج
tariiq muta'arrij
broken / uneven surface

الطريق مغلق
at-tariiq mughlaq
road closed

طريق ضيق
tariiq dayyiq
narrowing in the road

إبق على اليسار/اليمين
ibqa 'alaa al-yasaar / al-yamiin
keep right / left

الطريق مقفل
at-tariiq muqfal
road blocked

نفق
nafaq
tunnel

خروج
khuruuj
exit

السرعة القصوى
as-sur'a al-quswaa
maximum speed

ممر مقطوع/ممر مسدود امام
  للمترجلين
mamarr maqtuu' / mamarr
  masduud amaama al-
  mutarajjiliin
no access / no pedestrian
  access

ممنوع إيقاف السيارات
mamnuu' 'iiqaaf as-sayyaaraat
no hitchhiking

ممنوع الإنعطاف يمينا أو يسارا
mamnuu' al-in'itaaf yamiinan
  aw yasaaran
no right or left turn

دائرة قرصية
daa'ira qursiyya
disk zone

ستسحب السيارات في هذه المنطقة
sa-tushab as-sayyaaraat fii
  haadhihi l-mintaqa
tow-away area (both sides of
  the road)

The parts of a car
(The diagram shows the numbered parts)

1	battery	بطارية	battariyya
2	rear light	الضوء الخلفي	ad-daw'u al-khalfiy
3	rear-view mirror	المرآة الخلفية	al-mir'aat al-khalfiyya
	backup light	الضوء الإحتياطي	ad-daw'u al-ihtiyaatiy
4	aerial	الهوائي	al-hawaa'ii
	car radio	راديو السيارة	radyu as-sayyara
5	gas tank	خزان الوقود	khazzan al-waquud
6	spark plugs	شمعات القدح	shama'aat al-qadh
	fuel pump	مضخة الوقود	madakhat al-waquud
7	side mirror	المرآة الجانبية	al-mir'aat al-jaanibiyya
8	bumper	مخفف الصدمة	mukhaffif as-sadma
	carburetor	جهاز مزج الوقود (كبريتر)	jihaaz mazj al-waquud (kabraytar)
	crankcase	علبة التدوير	'ulbat at-tadwiir
	cylinder	أسطوانة	istuwaana
	ignition	قدح	qadh
	warning light	ضوء تحذير	daw' tahdhiir
	generator	مولد	muwallid
	accelerator	دواسة السرعة	dawwaasat as-sur'a
	handbrake	الفرامل اليدوية	al-faraamil al-yadawiyya
	valve	صمام	sammam
9	muffler	كمامة	kamaama
10	trunk	صندوق السيارة	sunduuq as-sayyaara
11	headlight	الضوء الأمامي	ad-daw'u al-amaami
	crank shaft	عمود المحرك	'amuud al-muharrik
12	air filter	مصفاة الهواء	misfaat al-hawaa'
	fog lamp	مصباح ضباب	misbaah dabaab
13	engine block	كتلة المحرك	kutlat al-muharrik
	camshaft	عمود الحدبات	'amuud al-hadabaat
	oil filter / pump	مصفاة زيت	misfaat zayt
	dipstick	الخطرة/مقياس الزيت	al-khatra / miqyas az-sayt
	pedal	دواسة	dawwaasa
14	door	باب	baab
15	radiator	راديتر	radaytar
16	brake disc	قرص الفرامل	qurs al-faraamil
	spare wheel	عجلة احتياطية	'ajalat ihtiyaatiyya
17	indicator	مؤشر	mu'ashir
18	windshield wiper	ماسحة	maasiha
19	shock absorbers	واقيات التعثر	waaqiyaat at-ta'athur
	sunroof	سقف السيارة	saqf as-sayyaara
	spoiler	اللوحة الخلفية للسيارة	al-lawhat al-khalfiya lis-sayyaara
20	steering column	عمود المقود	'amuud al-miqwad
	steering wheel	المقود	al-miqwad
21	exhaust pipe	أنبوب الدخان	unbuub ad-dukhaan
22	seat belt	حزام الأمان	hizaam al-'amaan

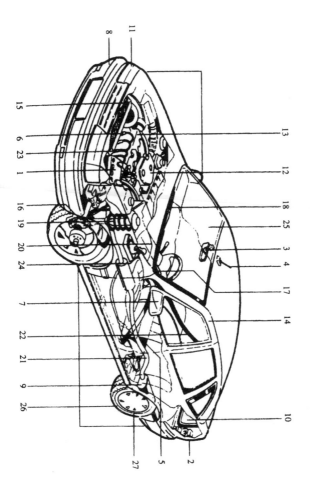

	fan	مروحة mirwaha
23	distributor cables	موزع أسلاك muwazzi' aslaak
24	gear shift	محول السرعة muhawwil as-sur'a
25	windshield	الزجاجة الامامية az-zujaaja l-amaamiyya
	water pump	مضخة الماء midakhat al-maa'
26	wheel	العجلة al-'ajala
27	hubcap	غطاء واقي ghitaa' waqii
	piston	مكبس mikbas

See the diagram on page 65

• Speed limits
On freeways 110 km/h for cars; on all main, non-urban highways 100 km/h; on secondary, non-urban highways 80 km/h; in built-up areas 50 km/h.
Give way to vehicles coming from the right unless otherwise indicated.
Towing prohibited to private drivers.

5.6 The gas station

• The cost of gas in the Middle East varies from one country to another but surprisingly high (around $1 per 1 liter), slightly less for unleaded.

How many kilometers to ___ the next gas station, please?	لو سمحت كم كيلومترا تبعد محطة البنزين القادمة؟ Law samahta kam kiilumitr tab'ud mahattat al-banziin al-qaadima?
I'd like...liters of... _____	أريد...ليترا من uriidu...litran min...
- super _____	رفيع rafii'
- leaded _____	مخلوط makhluut
- unleaded _____	بدون رصاص biduun rasaas
- diesel _____	ديزل diizil
...dollars worth of gas ___	...ما قيمته من البنزين ...maa qiimatuhu min l-banziin
Fill it up, please _____	إملأ هنا من فضلك imla' hunaa min fadlik
Could you check...? _____	هل يمكن أن تفحص...؟ hal yumkin an tafhasa...?
- the oil level _____	مستوى الزيت mustawaa az-zayt
- the tire pressure _____	ضغط الهواء في العجلات daght al-hawaa' fii l-'ajalaat
Could you change the oil, ___ please?	هل يمكن أن تغير الزيت من فضلك؟ hal yumkin an tughayyira az-zayt min fadlik?

On the road

66

Could you clean the _____ windshield, please?

هل تنظف الزجاجة الامامية من فضلك؟
hal tunazzif az-zujaaja al-amaamiyya min fadlik?

Could you wash the car, _____ please?

هل تغسل لي السيارة من فضلك؟
hal taghsil lii as-sayyaara min fadlik?

5.7 Breakdown and repairs

I have broken down, could ____ you give me a hand?

تعطلت سيارتي ممكن تساعدني من فضلك؟
taattalat sayyaaratii, mumkin tusaa'idunii min fadlik?

I've run out of gas _____

ليس لدي بنزين/نفذ لدي البنزين
laysa ladayya banziin / nafadha ladayya al-banziin

I've locked the keys in the ___ car

اقفلت السيارة وفيها المفاتيح
aqfaltu as-sayyaara wa fiihaa al-miftaah

The car / motorbike / _____ moped won't start

سيارتي/دراجتي/لا تشتغل (لا تعمل)
sayyaaratii / darraajatii / laa tashtaghil (laa ta'mal)

Could you contact the _____ breakdown service for me, please?

هل يمكن ان تتصل بخدمة الصيانة من فضلك؟
hal yumkin an tattasila bikhidmat as-siyaana min fadlik?

Could you call a garage _____ for me, please?

هل يمكن ان تتصل بورشة تصليح من فضلك؟
hal yumkin an tattasil biwarshat tasliih min fadlik?

Could you give me a lift _____ to...?

هل يمكن أن توصلني بسيارتك إلى... من فضلك؟
hal yumkin an tuusilanii bisayyaaratik illa...min fadlik?

- to the nearest garage? _____

إلى اقرب ورشة تصليح؟
ilaa aqrab warshat tasliih?

- to the nearest town? _____

إلى اقرب مدينة؟
ilaa aqrab madiina?

- to the nearest telephone _____ booth?

إلى اقرب هاتف عمومي؟
ilaa aqrab haatif 'umuumii?

- to the nearest emergency ___ phone?

إلى اقرب هاتف طوارىء؟
ilaa aqrab haatif tawaari'?

Can we take my moped? _____

هل يمكن ان نأخذ دراجتي؟
hal yumkin an na'khudha darraajatii?

5

On the road

| Could you tow me to a _____ garage? | هل يمكن ان تسحب سيارتي إلى اقرب ورشة تصليح؟ |
| | hal yumkin an tashaba sayyaaratii ilaa aqrab warshat tasliih? |

| There's probably something _____ wrong with... (See 5.5) | ربما تكون هناك مشكلة في لـ ... |
| | rubbamaa takuun hunaaka mushkila fii al-... |

| Can you fix it? _____ | هل تستطيع ان تصلحها ؟ |
| | hal tastatii tuslihaha? |

| Could you fix my tire? _____ | هل يمكنك ان تصلح عجلتي/دولابي ؟ |
| | hal yumkin an tusliha ajaltii (duulabii)? |

| Could you change this _____ wheel? | هل يمكن ان تغير هذا الدولاب ؟ |
| | hal yumkin an tughayyira haadha d-duulaab? |

| Can you fix it so it'll get _____ me to...? | هل يمكن اصلاحه بحيث يوصلني إلى...؟ |
| | hal yumkin islaahuhu bihaythu yuusilunii ilaa...? |

| Which garage can help _____ me? | اية ورشة تصليح يمكن ان تساعدني ؟ |
| | ayyatu warshat tasliih yumkin an tusaa'idanii? |

| When will my car / bicycle ___ be ready? | متى ستكون سيارتي/دراجتي جاهزة ؟ |
| | mata satakuun sayyaaratii / darraajatii jaahiza? |

| Have you already finished? _ | هل انتهيت؟ |
| | hal intahayta? |

| Can I wait for it here? _____ | هل يمكن ان انتظر هنا ؟ |
| | hal yumkin an antazira hunaa? |

| How much will it cost? _____ | كم سيكلف اصلاحها ؟ |
| | kam sayukallif islaahuhaa? |

| Could you itemize the bill? ___ | هل يمكن أن تكتب الفاتورة بالتفصيل ؟ |
| | hal yumkin an taktuba al-faatuura bit-tafsiil? |

| Could you give me a receipt _ for insurance purposes? | هل يمكن ان تعطيني وصلا بذلك ؟ |
| | hal yumkin an tu'tiyanii waslan bi-dhaalik? |

5 .8 The bicycle / moped

See the diagram on page 71

Bicycle paths are rare in the Middle East and, therefore, not much consideration for bikes should be expected on the roads. The maximum speed for mopeds is 40 km/h but you should be aged 14 and over. A crash helmet is compulsory up to the age of 18, and a new law is being considered to make helmets compulsory for anyone. This should be checked when you arrive.

لا — توجد لدي قطع غيار لـسيارتك/ دراجتك	I don't have parts for your car / bicycle
laa tuujad ladayya qita' li-sayyaaratik / darrajatik	
يجب ان اجلب القطع من مكان اخر	I have to get the parts from somewhere else
yajib an ajlaba l-qita' min makaanin aakhar	
يجب أن اطلب القطع	I have to order the parts
yajib an atluba l-qita'	
هذا يحتاج إلى نصف يوم	That'll take half a day
haadhaa yahtaaj ilaa nisf yawm	
هذا يحتاج إلى يوم كامل	That'll take a day
haadhaa yahtaaj ilaa yawm kaamil	
هذا يحتاج إلى بضعة أيام	That'll take a few days
haadhaa yahtaaj ilaa bid'at ayyaam	
هذا يحتاج إلى أسبوع	That'll take a week
haadhaa yahtaaj ilaa usbuu'	
سيارتك ستعوضها شركة التأمين	Your car is a write-off
sayyaaratuka sa-tu'awwiduhaa sharikatu t-ta'miin	
لا يمكن إصلاحها	It can't be repaired
laa yumkin islaahuhaa	
السيارة/الدراجة النارية/الدراجة الآلية/ الدراجة ستكون حاضرة الساعة...	The car / motor bike / moped / bicycle will be ready at...o'clock
as-sayyaara / ad-darraja an-naariyya / ad-darraja al-aaliyya / ad-darraja sa-takuun haadira as-saa'a...	

5 On the road

5 .9 Renting a vehicle

I'd like to rent a...	أريد ان استأجر...
	uriidu an asta'jira...
Do I need a (special) license for that?	هل احتاج إلى رخصة قيادة خاصة لذلك؟
	hal ahtaaju ilaa rukhsat qiyaada khaassa li-dhaalik?
I'd like to rent the...for...	أريد ان استأجر الـ...لمدة...
	uriidu an asta'jir al-...li-muddat ...
- the...for a day	الـ...ليوم واحد
	al-...li-yawmin waahid

69

The parts of a bicycle
(The diagram shows the numbered parts)

1 rear light _____ الإضاءة الخلفية al-idaa'a l-khalfiyya
2 rear wheel _____ العجلة الخلفية al-'ajala al-khalfiyya
3 (luggage) carrier _ حمال hammal
4 fork _____ عمود 'amuud
5 bell _____ جرس jaras
6 pedal crank _____ ذراع الدواسة dhiraa ad-dawwaasa
7 gear change _____ تغيير السرعة taghyiir as-sur'a
   wire _____ سلك silk
   generator _____ مولد muwwallid
   bicycle trailer _____ عربة مجرورة بدراجة 'araba majruura bi-darraja
   frame _____ إطار itaar
8 wheel guard _____ واقية العجلة waaqiyat al-'ajala
9 chain _____ سلسلة silsila
   chain guard _____ واقي السلسلة waaqii as-silsila
   odometer _____ عداد المسافة 'addad al-masaafa
   child's seat _____ مقعد أطفال maq'ad atfaal
10 headlight _____ الاضاءة الامامية al-idaa'a al-amaamiyya
   bulb _____ مصباح misbaah
11 pedal _____ دواسة dawwaasa
12 pump _____ مضخة midakha
13 reflector _____ العاكس al-'aakis
14 brake shoe _____ دواسة الفرامل dawwaasat al-faraamil
15 brake cable _____ سلك الفرامل silk al-faraamil
16 anti-theft device __ منبه ضد السرقة munabbih did as-sariqa
17 carrier straps ____ الأحزمة الناقلة al-ahzima an-naaqila
   tachometer _____ مقياس سرعة الدوران miqyaas sur'at ad-dawaraan
18 spoke _____ شعاع الدولاب shu'aa' ad-duulaab
19 mudguard _____ واقية waaqiya
20 handlebar _____ مقود الدراجة miqwad ad-darraja
21 chain wheel _____ السلسة الدولابية as-silsila ad-dulaabiya
   toe clip _____ مشبك الجر mishbak al-jarr
22 crank axle _____ محور التدوير mihwar at-tadwiir
   drum brake _____ إسطوانة الفرامل istiwaanat al-faraamil
23 rim _____ حافة haaffat
24 valve _____ صمام sammaam
25 gear cable _____ سلك مغير السرعة silk mughayir as-sur'a

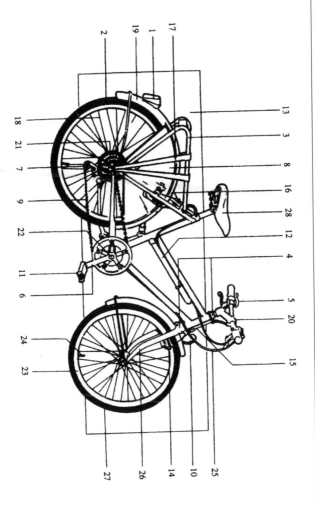

26 fork عمود 'amuud

27 front wheel العجلة الامامية al-'ajala al-amaamiyya

28 seat مقعد maq'ad

- the...for two days _____	الـ...ليومين al-...li-yawmayn
How much is that per day / __ week?	كم الاجرة لليوم الواحد/الاسبوع؟ kam al-ujra lil-yawm al-waahid / lil-'usbuu'?
How much is the deposit? __	كم يجب أن ادفع مقدما؟ kam yajibu an adfa'a muqaddaman?
Could I have a receipt for _____ the deposit?	هل يمكن أن تعطيني وصلا بالمبلغ المدفوع؟ hal yumkin an tu'tiyanii waslan bil-mablagh al-madfuu'?
How much is the surcharge __ per kilometer?	كم الاجرة الاضافية لكل كيلومتر؟ kam al-ujra al-idaafiyya likul kiilumitr?
Does that include gas? _____	هل هذا يشمل البنزين؟ hal haadhaa yashmal al-banziin?
Does that include _____ insurance?	هل هذا يشمل رسوم التأمين؟ hal haadhaa yashmal rusuum at-ta'miin?
What time can I pick the _____ ...up?	متى يمكن أن آخذ الـ...؟ mataa yumkin an aakhudha al-...?
When does it have to be _____ back?	متى يجب أن أعيد؟ mataa yajib an u'iida?
Where's the gas tank? _____	أين خزان البنزين؟ ayna khazzan al-banziin?
What sort of fuel does _____ it take?	ما نوع بنزين سيارتك؟ maa naw'u banziin sayyaratik?

5.10 Hitchhiking

Where are you heading?_____	إلى أين انت ذاهب؟ ilaa ayna anta dhaahib?
Can you give me a lift? _____	هل يمكن أن توصلني بسيارتك؟ hal yumkin an tuusilanii bi-sayyaritik?
Can my friend (f) come too? _	هل تستطيع صديقتي أن تأتي معي؟ hal tastatii'u sadiiqatii an ta'tiya ma'ii?
Can my friend (m) come _____ too?	هل يستطيع صديقتي أن يأتي معي؟ hal yastatii'u sadiiqii an ya'tiya ma'ii?
I'd like to go to... _____	أريد أن أذهب إلى... uriidu an adhhaba ilaa...
Is that on the way to...? _____	هل هذا هو الطريق إلى...؟ hal haadhaa huwa at-tariiq ilaa...?

Could you drop me off? _____	هل يمكن أن تنزلني عند ؟ hal yumkin an tunzilanii 'inda?
Could you drop me off _____ here?	هل يمكن أن تنزلني هذا ؟ hal yumkin an tunzilanii hunaa?
- at the entrance to the _____ highway?	عند مدخل الطريق السيارة ؟ 'inda madkhal at-tariiq as-sayyaara?
- in the center? _____	وسط المدينة؟ wasat al-madiina?
- at the next intersection? _____	عند التقاطع القادم ؟ 'inda at-taqaat'u al-qaadim?
Could you stop here, _____ please?	هل يمكن أن تتوقف هنا من فضلك ؟ hal yumkin an tatawaqqafa hunaa min fadlik?
I'd like to get out here _____	أريد أن أنزل هنا uriidu an anzila hunaa
Thanks for the lift _____	شكرا على المساعدة shukran 'alaa al-musaa'ada

Public transportation

6 **P**ublic transportation

6.1 In general

• Bus tickets are purchased at bus stations or on board the bus, and must be shown to the conductor when required. Single tickets can be bought in blocks of four.

قطار الساعة...المتوجه إلى... تأخر...دقائق qitaar as-sa'aa...al-mutawajjih ilaa ...ta'akhar...daqaa'iq	The [time] train to...has been delayed by... minutes
القطار المتوجه إلى...يصل الان إلى الرصيف... al-qitaar al-mutawajjih ilaa...yasil al-'aan ilaa r-rasiif...	The train to...is now arriving at platform...
القطار القادم من...يصل الان الى الرصيف... al-qitaar al-qaadim min...yasil ilaa r-rasiif...	The train from...is now arriving at platform...
القطار المتوجه إلى...سيغادر من الرصيف... al-qitaar al-mutawajjih ilaa... sayughaadir mina r-rasiif...	The train to...will leave from platform...
قطار الساعة...المتوجه إلى...سوف يغادر اليوم من الرصيف... qitaar as-sa'aa...al-mutawajjih ilaa...sawfa yughaadir l-yaum mina r-rasiif...	Today the [time] train to... will leave from platform...
المحطة القادمة هي... al-mahatta al-qaadima hiya...	The next station is...

Where does this train go to?	إلى أين يذهب هذا القطار؟ ilaa ayna yadhhab haadha l-qitaar?
Does this boat go to...?	هل هذا المركب ذاهب إلى...؟ hal haadha al-markab dhaahib ilaa...?
Can I take this bus to...?	هل استطيع ان اركب هذا الباص إلى...؟ hal astatii' an arkaba haadha al-baas ilaa...?
Does this train stop at...?	هل يتوقف هذا القطار عند...؟ hal yatawaqqaf haadha al-qitaar 'inda...?
Is this seat taken / free?	هل هذا المقعد محجوز/فارغ؟ hal haadha al-maq'ad mahjuuz / faarigh?

6

Public transportation

75

I've reserved... _____
انا لدي حجز...
anaa ladyya ḥajz...

Could you tell me where _____
I have to get off for...?
هل تستطيع ان تخبرني اين يجب ان انزل إلى...؟
hal tastaṭii' an tukhbiranii ayna yajibu an anzila ilaa...?

Could you let me know _____
when we get to...?
هل يمكن ان تخبرني عندما نصل إلى...؟
hal yumkin an tukhbiranii 'indamaa naṣil ilaa...?

Could you stop at the next _____
stop, please?
هل يمكن ان تتوقف عند الموقف القادم، من فضلك؟
hal yumkin an tatawaqqaf 'inda al-mawqif al-qaadim, min faḍlik?

Where are we? _____
أين نحن الآن؟
ayna naḥnu al-aan?

Do I have to get off here? _____
هل يجب ان انزل هنا؟
hal yajibu an anzila hunaa?

Have we already passed...? _____
هل تجاوزنا/عبرنا...؟
hal tajaawaznaa / 'abarnaa...?

How long have I been _____
asleep?
منذ متى انا نائم؟
mundhu mataa anaa naa'im?

How long does the train _____
stop here?
هل سيتوقف القطار طويلا هنا؟
hal sa-yatawaqqaf al-qiṭaar ṭawiilan hunaa?

Can I come back on the _____
same ticket?
هل يمكن ان اعود بنفس التذكرة؟
hal yumkin an a'uuda binafs at-tadhkira?

Can I change on this ticket? _____
هل يمكن ان أغير هذه التذكرة؟
hal yumkin an ughayyira haadhihi at-tadhkira?

How long is this ticket _____
valid for?
ما مدة صلاحية هذه التذكرة؟
maa muddat salaaḥiyyat haadhihi t-tadhkira?

How much is the extra fare _____
for the high-speed train?
ما الاجرة الاضافية للقطار السريع؟
maa l-ujra al-iḍaafiyya lil-qiṭaar as-sarii'?

Ticket types

درجة اولى ام ثانية؟ daraja uulaa am <u>th</u>aaniya?	First or second class?
رحلة واحدة ام ذهاب وایاب؟ rihla waa<u>h</u>ida am <u>dh</u>ahaab wa iyaab?	Single or return?
للمدخنين ام غير المدخنين؟ lil-muda<u>kh</u>iniin am <u>gh</u>ayr al-muda<u>kh</u>iniin?	Smoking or non-smoking?
مقعد بقرب الشباك؟ maq'ad biqurb a<u>sh</u>-<u>sh</u>ubbak?	Window or aisle seat?
في مقدمة ام نهاية القطار؟ fii muqaddimat am nihaayat al-qitaar?	Front or back (of train)?
مقعد او سرير؟ maq'ad aw sariir?	Seat or berth?
الأعلى، في الوسط ام في الأسفل؟ fii l-a'laa, fii al-wasat am fii l-asfal?	Top, middle or bottom?
درجة سياحية او درجة اولى؟ daraja syaahiya aw daraja uulaa?	Economy or first class?
حجرة او مقعد؟ hujra aw maq'ad?	Cabin or seat?
مفرد او مزدوج؟ mufrad aw muzdawaj?	Single or double?
كم عدد المسافرين؟ kam 'adadu l-musaafiriin?	How many are traveling?

Destination

اين تريد السفر؟ ayna turiidu s-safar?	Where are you travelling?
متى تريد السفر؟ mataa turiidu s-safar?	When are you leaving?
...ك يغادر الساعة... ...ka yu<u>gh</u>aadir as-sa'aa...	Your...leaves at...
عليك أن تغير 'alayka an tu<u>gh</u>ayyira	You have to change
عليك أن تنزل عند... 'alayka an tanzila 'inda...	You have to get off at...

6

Public transportation

عليك أن تذهب عبر... _____ You have to go via...
'alayka an tadhhaba 'abra...

رحلة الذهاب تكون... _____ The outward journey is on...
rihlat adh-dhahaab takuun...

رحلة الاياب (العودة) تكون... _____ The return journey is on...
rihlat al-iyaab (al-'awda) takuun...

يجب أن تركبا على الساعة... _____ You have to be on board by
yajib an tarkaba 'alaa s-saa'a...   ...(o'clock)

Inside the vehicle

تذاكر السفر من فضلك _____ Tickets, please
tadhaakir as-safar min fadlik

الحجز من فضلك _____ Your reservation, please
al-hajz min fadlik

جواز سفرك من فضلك _____ Your passport, please
jawaaz safarika min fadlik

انت في المقعد الخطأ _____ You're in the wrong seat
anta fii al-maq'ad al-khata'

انت مخطئ/انت في الـ...الخطأ _____ You have made a mistake /
anta mukhti' / anta fii al-...al-khata'   You are in the wrong...

هذا المقعد محجوز _____ This seat is reserved
haadhaa al-maq'ad mahjuuz

عليك ان تدفع اجرة اضافية _____ You'll have to pay extra
'alayka an tadfa' ujratan idaafiyya

الـ...تأخر...دقائق _____ The...has been delayed by...
al-...ta'akhar...daqaa'iq   minutes

6.3 Tickets

Where can I...? _____ اين يمكنني ان...؟
ayna yumkinunii an...?

- buy a ticket _____ اشتري تذكرة
ashtarii tadhkira

- reserve a seat _____ احجز مقعد
ahjiz maq'ad

- book a flight _____ احجز رحلة طيران
ahjiz rihlat tayaraan

Could I have...fo..., _____ هل يمكن ان احصل على...لـ...من
please?   فضلك؟
hal yumkin an ahsal 'alaa...li...min
fadlik?

A single, please _____	تذكرة رحلة واحدة من فضلك tadhkirat rihla waahida min fadlik
A return ticket, please _____	تذكرة ذهاب وإياب من فضلك tadhkirat dhahaab wa iyaab min fadlik
- first class _____	درجة اولى daraja uulaa
- second class _____	درجة ثانية daraja thaaniya
- economy class _____	درجة سياحية daraja siyaahiya
I'd like to reserve a seat / _____ berth / cabin	اريد ان احجز مقعدا/سريرا/حجرة uriidu an ahjiza maq'adan / sariiran/ hujratan
I'd like to reserve a top / _____ middle / bottom berth in the sleeping car	اريد ان احجز سريرا في الاعلى/الوسط/ الاسفل في عربة النوم uriidu an ahjiza sariiran fii al-'alaa / al-wasat / al-asfal fii 'arabat an-nawm
Smoking or non-smoking? _____	للمدخنين ام غير المدخنين؟ lil-mudakhiniin am ghayr al-mudakhiniin?
- by the window _____	قرب الشباك qurb ash-shubbaak
- single / double _____	مفرد/مزدوج mufrad / muzdawaj
- at the front / back _____	في المقدمة/المؤخرة fii al-muqaddima / al-mu'akhara
There are...of us _____	نحن...فردا nahnu...fardan
We have a car _____	لدينا سيارة ladaynaa sayyaara
We have a trailer _____	لدينا عربة صغيرة ladaynaa 'araba saghiira
We have...bicycles _____	لدينا...دراجات هوائية ladaynaa...darrajaat hawa'iyya
Do you have a...? _____	هل لديك...؟ hal ladayka...?
- travel card for 10 trips? _____	تذكرة سفر لعشر رحلات؟ tadhkirat safar li'ashar rahalaat?
- weekly travel card? _____	تذكرة سفر اسبوعية؟ tadhkirat safar usbuu'iyya?

6

Public transportation

| monthly season ticket? _____ | تذكرة سفر شهرية؟ |
| | tadhkirat safar <u>sh</u>ahriyya? |

| Where's...? _____ | اين ...؟ |
| | ayna ...? |

| Where's the information _____ desk? | اين مكتب المعلومات؟ |
| | ayna maktabu l-ma'luumaat? |

6.4 Information

| Where can I find a _____ schedule? | اين اجد جدولا بالمواعيد؟ |
| | ayna ajidu jadwalan bil-mawaa'iid? |

| Where's the...desk? _____ | اين مكتب الـ...؟ |
| | ayna maktab al...? |

| Do you have a city map _____ with the bus routes on it? | هل لديك خارطة للمدينة تحتوي على خطوط الباصات؟ |
| | hal ladayka <u>kh</u>aarita lilmadiina tahtawii 'alaa <u>kh</u>utuut al-baasaat? |

| Do you have a schedule? _____ | هل لديك قائمة بالمواعيد |
| | hal ladayka qaa'ima bilmawaa'iid? |

| Will I get my money back? _____ | هل سأسترجع نقودي؟ |
| | hal sa-'astarji'u nuquudii? |

| I'd like to confirm / cancel / _____ change my reservation for trip to... | اريد ان اؤكد/الغي/اغير الحجز/الرحلة الى... |
| | uriidu an u'akkida / ul<u>gh</u>iya / u<u>gh</u>ayira l-<u>h</u>ajz / ar-ri<u>h</u>la ilaa... |

| I'd like to go to... _____ | اريد ان اذهب الى... |
| | uriidu an a<u>dhh</u>aba ilaa... |

| What is the quickest way _____ to get there? | ماهو اسرع طريق للوصول الى هناك؟ |
| | maa huwa asra' <u>t</u>ariiq lil-wu<u>s</u>uul ilaa hunaak? |

| How much is a single / _____ return to...? | كم سعر رحلة واحدة/رحلة ذهاب واياب الى...؟ |
| | kam si'r ri<u>h</u>la waa<u>h</u>ida/ ri<u>h</u>la <u>dh</u>ahaab wa iyaab ilaa ...? |

| Do I have to pay extra? _____ | هل يجب ان ادفع اجورا اضافية؟ |
| | hal yajib an adfa' ujuuran i<u>d</u>aafiyya? |

| Can I break my journey _____ with this ticket? | هل يمكن ان اتوقف في مكان ما بهذه التذكرة؟ |
| | hal yumkin an atawaqqafa fii makaanin maa bi-haa<u>dh</u>ihi at-ta<u>dh</u>kira? |

How much luggage am I allowed?	ماهو الحد المسموح به من الامتعة/ الحقائب؟ maa huwa al-had al-masmuuh bihi min al-amti'a / al-haqaa'ib?
Is this a direct train?	هل هذا قطار مباشر؟ hal haadhaa qitaar mubaashir?
Do I have to change?	هل علي ان اغيرا؟ hal 'alayya an ughayyira?
Where?	اين؟ ayna?
Does the plane stop anywhere?	هل تتوقف الطائرة في مكان ما؟ hal tatawaqqaf at-taa'ira fii makaanin maa?
Will there be any stop-overs?	هل سيكون هناك اي توقفات؟ hal sayakun hunaaka ayya t-tawaqqufaat?
Does the boat stop at any other ports on the way?	هل تتوقف الباخرة في بعض الموانيء خلال الرحلة؟ hal tatawaqqaf al-baakhira fii ba'd al-mawaani' khilaala r-rihla?
Does the train / bus stop at...?	هل يتوقف القطار /الباص عند...؟ hal yatawaqqaf al-qitaar / al-baas 'inda...?
Where do I get off?	اين انزل؟ ayna anzil?
Is there a connection to...?	هل هناك تكملة الى...؟ hal hunaaka takmila ilaa...?
How long do I have to wait?	ما هي مدة الإنتظار؟ maa hiya muddatu l-intizaar?
When does...leave?	متى يغادر...؟ mataa yughaadir...?
What time does the first / next / last...leave?	متى يغادر اول/ ثاني /اخر...؟ mataa yughaadir awwal / thaanii / aakhir...?
How long does it take?	كم تستغرق الرحلة؟ kam tastaghriq ar-rihla?
What time does...arrive in...?	متى يصل الـ...الى...؟ mataa yasil al-...ilaa...?
Where does the...to... leave from?	من اين يغادر...المتوجه الى...؟ min ayna yughaadir...al-muttawajjih ilaa...?

6

Public transportation

| Is this the train / bus...to...? | هل هذا القطار/الباص ...الى... ؟ _ |
| | hal haa<u>dh</u>aa al-qi<u>t</u>aar / al-baa<u>s</u>... ilaa...? |

6.5 Airplanes

On arrival at an Arabic airport (ma<u>t</u>aar), you will find the following signs:

تسليم الأمتعة	دولي	رحلات داخلية
tasliim al-amti'a	duwalii	ra<u>h</u>alaat daa<u>kh</u>iliyya
check-in	**international**	**domestic flights**
وصول	مغادرة	
wu<u>s</u>uul	mu<u>gh</u>aadara	
arrivals	**departures**	

6.6 Trains

Train travel in the Middle East is simple and cheap. There are national railway companies in all countries of the region which offer services to the major cities. Services differ from one country to another, but overall you can expect a reasonable service frequency which does not always run on time. Tickets must be punched from the train station and shown at the entrance to platforms.

6.7 Taxis

There are plenty of taxis in all major cities with the cost varying substantially between very low in countries such as Syria and expensive in others such as the Gulf states. Taxis can be found in stands, especially at train and bus stations, or you can order taxis from your hotel reception with a surcharge sometimes payable for extra luggage and / or special pick up.

للاجرة	محجوز	محطة سيارة الاجرة
li-l'ujra	ma<u>hj</u>uuz	ma<u>hatt</u>at sayyaaraat
for hire	**occupied**	al-ujra
		taxi stand

Taxi! _____	تاكسي
	taaksi!
Could you get me a taxi, ____ please?	هل يمكن ان تطلب لي تاكسي من فضلك؟
	hal yumkin an ta<u>t</u>luba lii taaksi min fa<u>d</u>lik?
Where can I find a taxi ____ around here?	اين يمكن ان احصل على تاكسي من هنا؟
	ayna yumkin an a<u>h</u>sula 'alaa taaksi min hunaa?
Could you take me to..., ____ please?	هل يمكن ان تاخذني الى...من فضلك؟
	hal yumkin an ta'<u>kh</u>u<u>dh</u>anii ilaa...min fa<u>d</u>lik?

Public transportation

6

Could you take me to this address, please?	هل يمكن ان تاخذني الى هذا العنوان من فضلك؟
	hal yumkin an ta'khudhanii ilaa haadhaa al-'unwaan min fadlik?
- to the...hotel, please	الى فندق...من فضلك
	ilaa fundiq...min fadlik
- to the town / city center, please	الى مركز المدينة من فضلك
	ilaa markadh al-madiina min fadlik
- to the station, please	الى المحطة من فضلك
	ilaa l-mahatta min fadlik
- to the airport, please	الى المطار من فضلك
	ilaa l-mataar min fadlik
How much is the trip to...?	كم تكلف الرحلة الى...؟
	kam tukallif ar-rihla ilaa...?
How far is it to...?	كم المسافة الى...؟
	kam al-masaafa ilaa...?
Could you turn on the meter, please?	هل يمكن ان تشغل العداد من فضلك؟
	hal yumkin an tushaghila al-'addad min fadlik?
I'm in a hurry	انا على عجلة
	anaa 'alaa 'ajala
Could you speed up / slow down a little?	هل يمكن ان تسرع/تخفف من السرعة
	hal yumkin an tusri'a / tukhaffifa mina s-sur'a?
Could you take a different route?	هل يمكن ان تسلك طريقا اخر؟
	hal yumkin an tasluka tariiqan aakhar?
I'd like to get out here, please	اريد ان انزل هنا من فضلك
	uriid an anzila hunaa min fadlik
Go...	تحرك/اذهب
	taharrak / idhhab
You have to go here	يجب ان تذهب من هنا
	yajibu an tadhhaba min hunaa
Go straight ahead	اذهب مباشرة
	idhhab mubaasharatan
Turn left	إنعطف الى اليسار
	in'atif ilaa l-yasaar
Turn right	إنعطف الى اليمين
	in'atif ilaa l-yamiin

This is it / We're here _____ هذا هو العنوان/لقد وصلنا
haadhaa huwa l-'unwaan / laqad
waṣalnaa

Could you wait a minute _____ هل تنتظرني دقيقة من فضلك؟
for me, please? hal tantaẓirunii daqiiqa min faḍlik?

Public transportation

7 Overnight accommodation

7 **O**vernight accommodation

7.1 **G**eneral

كم ستبقى هنا؟ kam satabqaa hunaa?	How long will you be staying?
إملأ هذه الاستمارة من فضلك imla' haadhihi l-istimaara min fadlik	Fill out this form, please
هل يمكن ان ارى جواز سفرك؟ hal yumkin an araa jawaaza safarik?	Could I see your passport?
احتاج الى تسبقة ahtaaju ilaa tasbiqa	I'll need a deposit
عليك ان تدفع مقدما 'alayka an tadfa' muqaddaman	You'll have to pay in advance

My name is...	اسمي... ismii...
I've made a reservation	لدي حجز ladayya hajz
How much is it per night / week / month?	كم اجرة الليلة/الأسبوع/الشهر؟ kam ujrat l-layla/ al-'usbuu' / ash-shahr?
We'll be staying at least... nights / weeks	سنبقى على الاقل...ليال/اسابيع sa-nabqaa 'alaa l-aqal...layaalin / asaabii'
We don't know yet	الى حد الان لا نعرف ilaa haddi l'aan laa na'rif
Do you allow pets (cats / dogs)?	هل تسمح باصطحاب حيوانات اليفة؟ hal tasmah bi-'istihaab haywaanaat aliifa?
What time does the gate / door open / close?	متى تفتح/تغلق البوابة/الباب؟ mataa taftah / tughliq al-bawaaba / al-baab?
Could you get me a taxi, please?	هل يمكن ان تطلب لي تاكسي من فضلك؟ hal yumkin an tatluba lii taaksi min fadlik?
Is there any mail for me?	هل هناك اي بريد لي؟ hal hunaak ay bariid lii?

See the diagram on page 89

يمكن ان تختار الموقع الذي تريده yumkin an takhtaara al-mawqi' alladhii turiiduhu	You can pick your own site
سنعطيك موقعا sa-nu'tiika mawqi'aan	You'll be allocated a site
هذا رقم موقعك haadhaa raqmu mawqi'ik	This is your site number
اربط هذا جيدا بسيارتك، من فضلك irbit haadhaa jayyidan bi- sayyaaratik, min fadlik	Please stick this firmly to your car
يجب ان لا تفقد هذه البطاقة yajib an laa tafqida haadhihi al- bitaaqa	You must not lose this card

Where's the manager?	اين المدير؟ ayna al-mudiir?
Are we allowed to camp here?	هل مسموح ان نخيم هنا؟ hal masmuuh an nukhayyima hunaa?
There are...of us and we have...tents	نحن...افراد، ولدينا...خيم nahnu...afraad, wa ladaynaa... khiyam
Can we pick our own site?	هل يمكن ان نختار الموقع الذي نريد؟ hal yumkin an nakhtaara al-mawqi'a alladhii nuriid?
Do you have a quiet spot for us?	هل لديك مكان هادئ لنا؟ hal ladayka makaan haadi' lanaa?
Do you have any other sites available?	هل تتوفر لديك مواقع اخرى؟ hal tatawaffar ladayka mawaaqi' ukhraa?
It's too windy / sunny / shady here.	ريح شديدة/شمس قوية/ظل كثيف/هنا riih shadiida / shams qawiyya / zil kathiif/ hunaa
It's too crowded here	هذا المكان مزدحم جدا haadhaa l-makaanu muzdahim jiddan
The ground's too hard / uneven	الارض صلبة جدا/متعرجة al-ard salba jiddan / muta'arrija
Do you have a level spot for the trailer?	هل لديك مكان للعربة؟ hal ladayka makaan lil-'araba?

7

Overnight accommodation

Camping equipment
(The diagram shows the numbered parts)

luggage space __ مكان الحقائب makaan al-haqaa'iib

can opener ____ مفتاح علب miftaah 'ulab

butane gas ____ غاز البوتان ghaaz al-buutaan

bottle _____ قنينة qanniina

1 pannier _____ سلة كبيرة salla kabiira

2 gas cooker ____ جهاز طهي jihaaz tahiy

3 groundsheet ____ غطاء الارض ghitaa' al-ard

hammer _____ مطرقة mitraqa

hammock _____ ارجوحة شبكية urjuuha shabakiyya

4 gas can _____ علبة غاز 'ulbat ghaaz

campfire _____ نار المخيم naar al-mukhayyam

5 folding chair ____ كرسي قابل للطوي kursi qaabil lit-tawii

6 insulated picnic box __ صندوق عازل sunduuq aazil

ice pack _____ كيس ثلج kiis thalj

compass _____ بوصلة bawsala

corkscrew _____ مفتاح قناني miftaah qanaani

7 airbed _____ الفراش الهوائي al-firaash al-hawaa'iy

8 airbed pump ____ منفاخ الفراش الهوائي minfaakh al-firaash al-hawaa'iy

9 awning _____ مظلة mizalla

10 sleeping bag ____ حقيبة نوم haqiibat nawm

11 saucepan _____ قدر صغير qidr saghiir

12 handle (pan) ____ اليد الماسكة al-yad al-maasika

primus stove ____ جهاز طهي صغير jihaaz tahiy saghiir

lighter _____ ولاعة/قداحة walla'a / qaddaha

13 backpack _____ حقيبة ظهر haqiibat zahr

14 guy rope _____ حبل habl

15 storm lantern ___ مصباح العاصفة misbaah al-'aasifa

camp bed _____ فراش مخيم firaash mukhayyam

table _____ طاولة taawila

16 tent _____ خيمة khayma

17 tent peg _____ وتد الخيمة watad al-khayma

18 tent pole _____ عمود الخيمة 'amuud al-khayma

thermos _____ ترمس tarmus

19 water bottle ____ قنينة ماء qinniinat maa'

clothes pin ____ مساك ملابس massaak malaabis

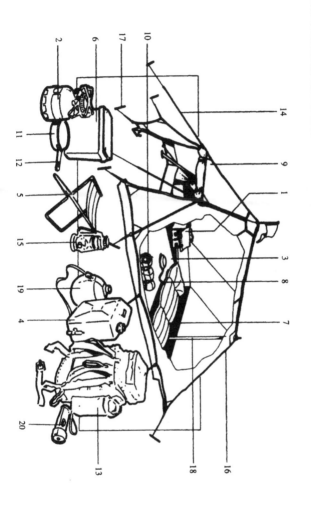

clothes line _____ حبل الغسيل <u>h</u>abl al-<u>gh</u>asiil	
windbreak _____ واقية من الريح waaqiya min ar-rii<u>h</u>	
20 flashlight _____ ضوء وامض <u>d</u>aw' waami<u>d</u>	
penknife _____ سكين قلم sikkiin qalam	

Could we have adjoining sites?	هل يمكن ان نحصل على مواقع متقاربة؟ hal yumkin an nahsula 'alaa mawaaqi'a mutaqaariba?
Can we park the car next to the tent?	هل يمكن ان نوقف السيارة قرب الخيمة؟ hal yumkin an nuuqifa as-sayyaara qurba al-khayma?
How much is it per person / tent / trailer / car?	كم الاجرة للفرد الواحد/للخيمة/للعربة/للسيارة؟ kam al-ujra lil-fard al-waahid / lil-khayma / lil-'araba / lis-sayyaara?
Do you have chalets for hire?	هل لديك بيت اصطياف للإيجار؟ hal ladayka bayt istiyaaf lil-'iijaar?
Are there any...?	هل هناك اي...؟ hal hunaaka ay...?
- hot showers	دش ساخن؟ dush saakhin
- washing machines	غسالة ghassaala
Is there a...on the site?	هل يوجد...في هذا المكان؟ hal yuujad...fii haadhaa al-makaan?
Is there a children's play area on the site?	هل توجد ساحة لعب للاطفال في هذا المكان؟ hal tuujad saahat la'ib lil-atfaal fii haadhaa al-makaan?
Are there covered cooking facilities on the site?	هل توجد تسهيلات طبخ مغطاة في هذا المكان؟ hal tuujad tashiilat tabkh mughattaat fii haadhaa al-makaan?
Can I rent a safe?	هل يمكن ان استأجر صندوق امانات؟ hal yumkin an asta'jjira sunduuq amaanaat?
Are we allowed to barbecue here?	هل يسمح لنا ان نشوي هنا؟ hal yusmahu lanaa an nashwiya hunaa?
Are there any power outlets?	هل توجد منافذ كهربائية؟ hal tuujad manaafidha kahrubaa'iyya?
Is there drinking water?	هل يوجد ماء شرب؟ hal yuujad maa' shurb?
When's the garbage collected?	متى يتم جمع الزبالة؟ mataa yatim jam' az-zibaala?
Do you sell gas bottles (butane gas / propane gas)?	هل تبيع قناني غاز؟ hal tabii' qanaani ghaaz?

Overnight accommodation

Do you have a single / _____
double room available?

هل تتوفر لديك غرفة لشخص/لشخصين؟

hal tatawaffar ladayka ghurfa
lishakhs / lishakhsayn?

- per person / per room _____

لكل شخص/لكل غرفة

ikul shakhs / likul ghurfa

Does that include breakfast / _
lunch / dinner?

هل هذا يشمل الافطار/الغداء/العشاء؟

hal haadhaa yashmal al-iftaar /
al-ghadaa' / al-'ashaa'?

Could we have two _____
adjoining rooms?

هل يمكن ان نحصل على غرفتين
متجاورتين؟

hal yumkin an nahsula 'alaa
ghurfatayn mutajaawiratayn?

- with / without toilet / _____
bath / shower

مع/بدون مرافق/حمام/دش

ma'a / biduun maraafiq / hammaam /
dush

- facing the street _____

مواجه للشارع

muwaajih lish-shaari'

- at the back _____

في الخلف

fii al-khalf

- with / without sea view _____

مع/بدون اطلالة على البحر

ma'a / biduun itlaala 'alaa al-bahr

Is there...in the hotel? _____

هل يوجد...في الفندق؟

hal yuujadu...fii al-fundiq?

Is there an elevator in the _____
hotel?

هل يوجد مصعد كهربائي في الفندق؟

hal yuujadu mis'ad kahrabaa'ii fii al-
fundiq?

Do you have room service? _

هل توفر خدمات للغرف؟

hal tuwaffir khadamaat lil-ghuraf?

Could I see the room? _____

هل يمكن ان ارى الغرفة؟

hal yumkin an araa al-ghurfa?

الحمام والمرافق في نفس الطابق/في
الغرفة

al-hammam wa al-maraafiq fii
nafs at-taabiq / fii l-ghurfa

— The toilet and shower are
on the same floor / in
the room

من هنا من فضلك

min hunaa min fadlik

— This way, please

غرفتك في الطابق...، رقم...

ghurfatuka fii at-taabiq...raqm...

— Your room is on the...
floor, number...

Overnight accommodation

91

I'll take this room _____ سآخذ هذه الغرفة
sa-aakhudh haadhihi al-ghurfa

We don't like this one _____ نحن لا نريد هذا
nahnu laa nuriidu haadha

Do you have a larger / less ___ هل لديك غرفة اكبر/ارخص؟
expensive room?
hal ladayka ghurfa akbar / arkhas?

Could you put in a cot? _____ هل يمكن ان تضع سرير أطفال؟
hal yumkin an tada'a sariir atfaal?

What time's breakfast? _____ متى وقت الافطار؟
mataa waqt al-'iftaar?

Where's the dining room? ___ اين غرفة الطعام؟
ayna ghurfat at-ta'aam?

Can I have breakfast in my __ هل يمكن ان اتناول فطوري في غرفتي؟
room?
hal yumkin an atanaawala fatuurii fii ghurfatii?

Where's the emergency _____ اين مخرج الطواريء/منفذ الحريق؟
exit / fire escape?
ayna makhraj at-tawaari' / manfadh al-hariiq?

Where can I park my car _____ أين يمكن ان أوقف سيارتي؟
safely?
ayna yumkin an uuqifa sayyaaratii?

The key to room..., please ___ مفتاح الغرفة...من فضلك
miftaah al-ghurfa...min fadlik

Could you put this in the ___ هل يمكن ان تحفظ لي هذا في الامانات
safe, please?
من فضلك؟
hal yumkin an tahfaza lii haadha fii al-amaanaat?

Could you wake me at... ____ هل يمكن ان توقظني الساعة...غدا؟
tomorrow?
hal yumkin an tuqizanii as-saa'a... ghadan?

Could you find a babysitter __ هل يمكن ان احصل على مربية أطفال؟
for me?
hal yumkin an ahsula 'alaa murabbiyat atfaal?

Could I have an extra _____ هل يمكن ان احصل على بطانية اضافية؟
blanket?
hal yumkin an ahsula 'alaa battaniyya idaafiyya?

What days do the cleaners __ في أي يوم يأتي المنظفون؟
come in?
fii ay yawm ya'tii al-munazzifuun?

When are the sheets / _____ متى يتم تغيير الشراشف/المناشف/
towels / dish towels
مناشف الحمام؟
changed?
mataa yatum taghyiir ash-sharaashif / al-manaashif / manaashif al-hammaam?

Overnight accommodation

We can't sleep for the noise	لا نستطيع ان ننام بسبب الضوضاء
	laa nastatii' an nanaama bi-sababi al-dawdaa'
Could you turn the radio down, please?	هل يمكن ان تخفض صوت المذياع (الراديو) من فضلك؟
	hal yumkin an takhfida' sawt al-midhyaa' (ar-raadiyuu) min fadlik?
We're out of toilet paper	لا توجد اوراق (كلينكس) في التواليت
	laa tuujad awraaq (kliiniks) fii at-tuwaaliit
There aren't any... / there's not enough...	لا يوجد هناك اي.../ لا يوجد...كافي
	laa yuujad hunaak ay... / laa yuujad... kaafii
The bed linen's dirty	أغطية الفراش وسخة
	aghtiyat al-firaash wasikha
The room hasn't been cleaned	الغرفة لم تنظف
	al-ghurfa lam tunazaf
The kitchen is not clean	المطبخ ليس نظيفا
	al-matbakh laysa naziifan
The kitchen utensils are dirty	أدوات المطبخ وسخة
	adawaat al-matbakh wasikha
The heating isn't working	التدفئة لا تعمل
	at-tadfi'a laa ta'mal
There's no hot water / electricity	لا يوجد ماء ساخن/كهرباء
	laa yuujad maa' saakhin / kahrabaa'
...doesn't work / is broken	الـ...لا يعمل/مكسور
	al-...laa ya'mal / maksuur
Could you have that seen too?	هل يمكن ان تفحص ذلك أيضا؟
	hal yumkin an tafhasa dhaalik aydan?
Could I have another room / site?	هل لديك غرفة/موقع اخر؟
	hal ladayka ghurfa / mawqi' aakhar?
The bed creaks terribly	الفراش يصدر صوتا مزعجا
	al-firaash yusdiru sawtan muz'ijan
The bed sags	الفراش يرتخي
	al-firaash yartakhii
Could I have a board under the mattress?	هل يمكن ان تضع خشبة تحت الفرشة؟
	hal yumkin an tada'a khashaba tahta al-farsha?

7 Overnight accommodation

It's too noisy _____	ضوضاء كبيرة
	<u>d</u>aw<u>d</u>aa' kabiira
There are a lot of insects ___	يوجد الكثير من الحشرات
	yuujad al-ka<u>th</u>iir min al-<u>h</u>asharaat
This place is full of _____ mosquitoes	هذا المكان مليء بالبعوض
	haa<u>dh</u>aa al-makaan malii' bil-ba'uud
- cockroaches _____	صراصير
	<u>s</u>araa<u>s</u>iir

7.5 Departures

See also 8.2 Settling the bill

I'm leaving tomorrow _____	سأغادر غدا
	sa-'u<u>gh</u>aadir <u>gh</u>adan
Could I pay my bill, please? __	الفاتورة من فضلك؟
	al-faatuura min fa<u>d</u>lik?
What time should we _____ check-out?	متى يجب أن نترك الغرفة؟
	mataa yajibu an natruka al-<u>gh</u>urfa?
Could I have my deposit / passport back, please?	هل يمكن ان استرجع الضمان/جواز سفري من فضلك؟
	hal yumkin an astarji'a a<u>d</u>-<u>d</u>amaan / jawaaza safarii min fa<u>d</u>lik?
We're in a big hurry _____	نحن مستعجلون جدا
	na<u>h</u>nu musta'jiluuna jiddan
Could you forward my mail __ to this address?	هل يمكن ان تحول بريدي الى هذا العنوان؟
	hal yumkin an tu<u>h</u>awwila bariiddii ilaa haa<u>dh</u>aa al-'unwaan?
Could we leave our _____ luggage here until we leave?	هل يمكن ان نترك حقائبنا هنا الى حين نغادر؟
	hal yumkin an natruk <u>h</u>aqaa'ibanaa hunaa ilaa <u>h</u>iin nu<u>gh</u>aadir?
Thanks for your hospitality __	شكرا على حسن الضيافة
	<u>sh</u>ukran 'alaa <u>h</u>usni a<u>d</u>-<u>d</u>iyaafa

Money matters

8 Money matters

• In general, banks are open to the public from 8.30a.m. to 12.30p.m., and 1.30 to 4.30p.m., but it is always possible to find an exchange office (*masraf*) open in larger towns or tourist centers. Proof of identity is usually required to exchange currency. Keep in mind that Friday, not Sunday, is the day off in most countries of the Middle East.

8.1 Banks

Where can I find a bank / an exchange office around here?	اين يمكن ان اجد مصرفا/مكتب تصريف عملة أجنبية هنا؟ ayna yumkin an ajida maṣrafan / maktab taṣriif 'umla ajnabiyya hunaa?
Where can I cash this traveler's check?	اين يمكن ان اصرف هذا الشيك؟ ayna yumkin an aṣrifa haadhaa ash-shiik?
Can I cash this here?	هل يمكن ان أصرف هذا هنا؟ hal yumkin an aṣrifa haadhaa hunaa?
Can I withdraw money on my credit card here?	هل يمكن ان اسحب بعض النقود هنا بواسطة بطاقة الاعتماد؟ hal yumkin an aṣhaba ba'da an-nuquud hunaa bi-waasiṭati biṭaaqat al-i'timaad?
What's the minimum / maximum amount?	ما هو اقصى/ادنى مبلغ؟ maa huwa aqṣaa / adnaa mablagh?
Can I take out less than that?	هل استطيع ان اسحب اقل من ذلك؟ hal astaṭii'u an aṣhaba aqalla min dhaalik?
I had some money cabled here	لقد ارسل مبلغ مالي لحسابي الى هنا laqad ursila mablagh maaliy li-ḥisaabii ilaa hunaa
Has it arrived yet?	هل وصل بعد؟ hal waṣala ba'du?
These are the details of my bank in the USA	هذه تفاصيل مصرفي في امريكا haadhihi tafaaṣiil maṣrafii fii amriika
This is the number of my bank / account	هذا رقم مصرفي/رقم حسابي haadhaa raqmu maṣrafii / raqmu ḥisaabii
I'd like to change some money	اريد ان احول (اصرف) بعض النقود uriid an uḥawwila (uṣarrifa) ba'da an-nuquud
- pounds into...	من الجنيه إلى... min al-jiniih ilaa...

– dollars into... _____	من الدولار إلى...
	min ad-duulaar ilaa...

What's the exchange rate? ___	ما هو سعر العملة؟
	maa huwa si'ru al-'umla?

Could you give me some ___ small change with it?	هل يمكن ان تعطيني بعض الفكة مع هذا؟
	hal yumkin an tu'tiyanii ba'd al-fakka ma'a haadha?

This is not right _____	هذا غير صحيح
	haadhaa ghayr sahiih

_____ Sign here, please	وقع هنا من فضلك
	waqqi' hunaa min fadlik

_____ Fill this out, please	إملأ هذا من فضلك
	imla' haadhaa min fadlik

– Could I see your passport, please?	هل يمكن ان ارى جواز سفرك من فضلك؟
	hal yumkin an araa jawaaza safarik min fadlik?

Could I see your identity card, please?	هل يمكن ان ارى بطاقتك الشخصية من فضلك؟
	hal yumkin an araa bitaaqataka ash-shakhsiyya min fadlik?

Could I see your check card, please?	هل يمكن ان ارى بطاقة التثبت من فضلك؟
	hal yumkin an araa bitaaqat at-tathabbut min fadlik?

Could I see your bank card, please?	هل استطيع ان ارى بطاقتك المصرفية من فضلك؟
	hal astatii'u an araa bitaaqatak al-masrafiyya min fadlik?

8.2 Settling the bill

Could you put it on my bill? _	هل يمكن ان تضيفه الى الفاتورة؟
	hal yumkin an tudiifahu ilaa al-faatuura?

Is the tip included? _____	هل الإكرامية (البقشيش) ضمن السعر؟
	hal ikraamiyya (al-baqshiish) dimn as-si'r?

Can I pay by...? _____	هل يمكن ان ادفع بواسطة...؟
	hal yumkin an adfa'a bi-waasitati...?

Can I pay by credit card? ____ هل يمكن ان ادفع بواسطة بطاقة اعتماد؟
hal yumkin an adfa'a bi-waasitati
bitaaqat i'timaad?

Can I pay by traveler's _____ هل استطيع الدفع بواسطة شيك سياحي؟
check? hal asatii' ad-daf' bi-waasitati shiik
siyaahii?

Can I pay with foreign ____ هل يمكن ان ادفع بالعملة الاجنبية؟
currency? hal yumkin an adfa'a bil-'umla al-
ajnabiyya?

You've given me too much / _ اعطيتني كثيرا/لم تعطني كل الباقي
you haven't given me a'ttaytanii kathiiran / lam tu'ttinii kul
enough change al-baaqii

Could you check this again, _ هل يمكن ان تتثبت مرة اخرى؟
please? hal yumkin an tatathabbata marratan
uhkhraa?

Could I have a receipt, _____ هل يمكن ان احصل على وصل؟
please? hal yumkin an ahsula 'alaa wasl?

I don't have enough money _ ليس معي نقود كافية
on me laysa ma'ii nuquud kaafiya

نحن لا نقبل بطاقات الاعتماد / _____ We don't accept credit
شيك سياحي/عملات اجنبية cards / traveler's checks /
nahnu laa naqbal bitaaqaat foreign currency
al-i'timaad / shiik siyaahii /
'umlaat ajnabiyya

This is for you _____ هذا لك
haadhaa laka

Keep the change _____ إحتفظ بالباقي
ihtafiz bil-baaqii

Mail and telephone

9 **M**ail and telephone

9.1 Mail

For banks, see 8 Money matters

• Major post offices are open Sunday to Thursday from 8.30 a.m. to 5.00 p.m. Stamps (*tawaabi'*) can also be purchased at authorized tobacconists (*dukkaan*). The cost of sending a letter depends on its weight and the cost of sending an airmail letter also depends on where it is being sent. Postal services in some countries in the Middle East are quite slow.

طوابع ṭawaabi' stamps	برقيات barqiyyaat telegrams	حوالة بريدية ḥawaala bariidiyya money orders
رزم ruzam parcels		

Where is...?	اين . . .	
	ayna...?	
- the nearest post office	أقرب مكتب بريد	
	aqrab maktab bariid	
- the main post office	مكتب البريد الرئيسي	
	maktab al-bariid ar-ra'iisii	
- the nearest mail box	أقرب صندوق بريد	
	aqrab ṣunduuq bariid	
Which counter should I go to?	الى اي شباك يجب ان اذهب لـ؟	
	ilaa ay shubbaak yajibu an adhhaba li?	
Which counter should I go to to send a fax?	الى اي شباك ان اذهب لإرسال فاكس؟	
	ilaa ay shubbaak yajibu an adhhaba li'irsaal faaks?	
Which counter should I go to to change money?	الى اي شباك يجب ان اذهب لتصريف بعض النقود؟	
	ilaa ay shubbaak yajibu an adhhaba litaṣriif ba'ḍ an-nuquud?	
Which counter should I go to to change giro checks?	الى اي شباك ان اذهب لتصريف هذا الشيك؟	
	ilaa ay shubbaak yajibu an adhhaba li-taṣriif haadhaa ash-shiik?	
Which counter should I go to to wire a money order?	الى اي شباك يجب ان اذهب لإرسال حوالة بريدية؟	
	ilaa ay shubbaak yajibu an adhhaba li'irsaal ḥawaala bariidiyya?	

100

Which counter should I go to for general delivery?	الى اي شباك يجب ان اذهب لتسلم الأمتعة ilaa ay <u>sh</u>ubbaak yajibu an a<u>dh</u>haba li-tasallum al-amti'a?
Is there any mail for me?	هل يوجد اي بريد لي hal yuujad ay bariid lii?
My name's...	اسمي... ismii...

Stamps

What's the postage for a... to...?	كم أجرة البريد لـ...الـ... kam ujrat al-bariid li...laa...?
Are there enough stamps on it?	هل فيها طوابع كافية؟ hal fiihaa <u>t</u>awaabi' kaafiya?
I'd like [quantity] [value] stamps	اريد ما قيمته...طوابع... uriidu maa qiimatuhu...<u>t</u>awaabi'...
I'd like to send this...	اريد ان ارسل هذه... uriidu an ursila haa<u>dh</u>ihi...
- by express	بالبريد السريع bi-lbariid as-sarii'
- by air mail	بالبريد الجوي bi-lbariid al-jawwii
- by registered mail	بالبريد المسجل bi-lbariid al-musajjal

Telegram / fax

I'd like to send a telegram to...	اريد ان ارسل برقية الى... uriidu an ursila barqiyya ilaa...
How much is that per word?	كم كلفة كل كلمة؟ kam kulfatu kull kalima?
This is the text I want to send	هذا هو النص الذي اريد ان ارسله haa<u>dh</u>aa huwa an-na<u>s</u> alla<u>dh</u>ii uriidu an ursilahu
Shall I fill out the form myself?	هل املأ الاستمارة بنفسي؟ hal amla'u al-istimaara binafsii?
Can I make photocopies / send a fax here?	هل يمكن ان اصور وثائق (فوتوكوبي) / ارسل فاكس من هنا؟ hal yumkin an u<u>s</u>awwira wa<u>th</u>aa'iqa (futukuubii) / ursil faaks min hunaa?
How much is it per page?	كم كلفة كل صفحة؟ kam kulfat kull <u>s</u>afha?

9 .2 Telephone

See also 1.8 Telephone alphabets

• Direct internasional calls can easily be made from public telephones using a phone card available from newspaper stands, and post offices and Telecom offices. Dial 00 to get out of the country, then the relevant country code (USA 1), city code and number. Collect phone calls are difficult to make and the fact that many operators do not speak English makes them even more inaccessible. When phoning someone in an Arab country, you will be greeted with "aaluu".

Is there a phone booth around here?	هل يوجد هاتف عمومي قريب من هنا ؟ hal yuujad haatif 'umuumii qariib min hunaa?
May I use your phone, please?	هل يمكن ان استخدم هاتفك؟ hal yumkin an astakhdima haatifak?
Do you have a city phone directory?	هل لديك دليل بأرقام هواتف المدينة ؟ hal ladayka daliil bi'arqaam hawaatif al-madiina?
Where can I get a phone card?	اين يمكن ان احصل على بطاقة تلفون؟ ayna yumkin an ahsula 'alaa bitaaqat tilifuun?
Could you give me...?	هل يمكن ان تعطيني...؟ hal yumkin an tu'tiyanii...?
- the number for international directory assistance	رقم المساعدة الدولي raqm al-musaa'da ad-duwalii
- the number of room...	رقم غرفة... raqm ghurfa...
- the international access code	المفتاح الدولي al-miftaah ad-duwalii
- the country code for...	مفتاح البلد... miftaah al-balad...
- the area code for...	مفتاح المنطقة... miftaah al-mintaqa...
- the number of... [subscriber]	رقم المشترك... raqamu al-mushtarik...
Could you check if this number's correct?	هل يمكن ان تتأكد ان هذا الرقم صحيح؟ hal yumkin an ta-ta'akkada anna haadhaa ar-raqm sahiih?
Can I dial international direct?	هل أستطيع ان اتصل بالخارج مباشرة؟ hal astatii'u an attasila bil-khaarij mubaasharatan?

Do I have to go through the switchboard?	هل يجب ان أتصل أولا بمركز الإتصالات؟ hal yajibu an attasila awwalan bi-markazi al-ittisaalaat?
Do I have to dial 0 first?	هل يجب ان ادور الرقم 0 أولا؟ hal yajibu an udawwira ar-raqm 0 awwalan?
Do I have to reserve my calls?	هل يجب ان احجز مكالماتي؟ hal yajibu an ahjiza mukaalamaatii?
Could you dial this number for me, please?	لو سمحت هل يمكن ان تطلب لي هذا الرقم؟ law samaht hal yumkin an tatluba lii haadhaa ar-raqm?
Could you put me through to... / extension..., please?	هل يمكن ان تحولني على.../الرقم الداخلي ...من فضلك؟ hal yumkin an tuhawwilanii 'alaa... / ar-raqam ad-dakhilii...min fadlik?
I'd like to place a collect call to...	اريد ان اقوم بمكالمة الى...على حساب المستلم uriidu an aquuma bi-mukaalama ilaa...'alaa hisaab al-mustalim
What's the charge per minute?	كم كلفة الدقيقة الواحدة؟ kam kulfat ad-daqiiqa al-waahida?
Have there been any calls for me?	هل وصلتني مكالمات هاتفية؟ hal wasalatnii mukaalamaat haatifiyya?

The conversation

Hello, this is...	آلو معك... aaluu ma'aka...
Who is this, please?	من على الخط؟ man 'alaa l-khat?
Is this...?	هل هذا...؟ hal haadha...?
I'm sorry, I've dialed the wrong number	انا آسف طلبت رقما خطأ anaa aasif, talabtu raqman khata'
I can't hear you	لا استطيع ان اسمعك laa astatii'u an asma'aka
I'd like to speak to...	اريد ان أتكلم مع... uriidu an atakallama ma'a...
Is there anybody who speaks English?	هل يوجد اي شخص يتكلم الانكليزية؟ hal yuujad ay shakhs yatakallam al-inkliiziyya?
Extension..., please	الرقم الداخلي...من فضلك ar-raqm ad-daakhilii...min fadlik

هناك مكالمة هاتفية لك — There's a phone call for you
hunaaka mukaalama haatifiyya laka

يجب ان تدور الرقم 0 أولا — You have to dial 0 first
Yajibu an tudawwira ar-raqm sifr
awwalan

لحظة من فضلك — One moment, please
lahza min fadlik

ليس هناك من يرد — There's no answer
laysa hunaaka man yarudd

الخط مشغول — The line's busy
al-khat mashghuul

هل تريد ان تبقى على الخط؟ — Do you want to hold?
hal turiid an tabqaa 'alaa al-khat?

احولك إلى — Connecting you
uhawwiluka ilaa

طلبت رقما خطأ — You've got a wrong number
talabt raqman khata'

هو غير موجود / هي غير موجودة في — He's / she's not here right now
الوقت الحاضر
huwa ghayr mawjuud / hiya ghayr
mawjuuda fii al-waqt al-haadir

هو سيعود / هي ستعود الساعة... — He'll / she'll be back at...
huwa sa-ya'uud / hiya sa-ta'uud
as-saa'a...

هذا جهاز الرد الآلي... — This is the answering machine of...
haadhaa jihaaz ar-radd al-aalii...

Could you ask him / her to call me back? — هل يمكن ان تطلب منه ان يتصل / هل يمكن ان تطلب منها أن تتصل بي؟
hal yumkin an tatluba minhu an yattasila / hal yumkin an tatluba minhaa an tattasila bii?

My name's... — اسمي...
ismii...

My number's... — رقمي هو...
raqmii huwa...

Could you tell him / her I called? — هل يمكن ان تخبره / تخبرها اني اتصلت؟
hal yumkin an tukhbirahu / tukhbirahaa annii ittasaltu?

I'll call him / her back tomorrow — سوف أتصل به / بها غدا
sawfa attasil bihi / bihaa ghadan

Shopping

10 Shopping

• Shops are generally open Saturday to Thursday from 9.00a.m. to 7.30p.m. Grocery shops may not re-open until 5.00p.m. and could stay open until 9.00p.m. in the summer. Shops, department stores and supermarkets usually close for a half day during the week – usually on Friday afternoons. Some variation across countries also exists as to the hours of business.

دكان بقالة
dukkaan baqaala
grocery shop

حلاق
hallaaq
barber's

مجوهرات أزياء
mujawharaat azyaa'
costume jewelry

دكان احذية
dukkaan ahdhiya
footwear

اسكافي
iskaafii
cobbler

دكان قرطاسية
dukkaan qurtaasiyya
stationery shop

بضائع منزلية
badaa'i' manziliyya
household goods

وكالة طباعة
wikaalat tibaa'a
typing agency

كشك لبيع الصحف
kushk li bay' as-suhuf
newsstand

مخزن خمور
makhzan khumuur
stock of vintage wines

محل آلي لتنظيف الملابس
mahal aalii li-tanziif al-malaabis
coin-operated laundry / dry cleaner

دكان لبيع الكتب
dukkaan libay' al-kutub
bookshop

جزار
jazzaar
butcher's shop

ورشة تصليح دراجات
warshat tasliih darraajaat
motorbike and bicycle repairs

سوق
suuq
market

محل لوازم الخياطة
mahal lawaazim al-khiyaata
haberdashery

دكان بضاعة مستعملة
dukkaan bidaa'a musta'mala
second-hand shop

دكان ملابس
dukkaan malaabis
clothing shop

دكان لوازم مخيم
dukkaan lawaazim mukhayyam
camping supplies shop

محل خضار وفواكه
mahal khudaar wa fawaakih
fruit and vegetable shop

دكان لبيع اللعب
dukkaan libay' al-lu'ab
toy shop

دكان الات موسيقية
dukkaan aalaat muusiiqiyya
musical instrument shop

دكان اخدم نفسك بنفسك
dukkaan ikhdim nafsak binafsik
do-it-yourself shop

دكان مجوهرات
dukkaan mujawharaat
goldsmith

ساعاتي
saa'aatii
watches and clocks

النظاراتي
an-nazzaaraatii
optician

مخبزة
makhbaza
baker's shop

حلاق
hallaaq
hairdresser

دكان حلويات
dukkaan halawiyyaat
confectioner's / cake shop

لوازم جلدية
lawaazim jildiyyah
leather goods

الفرائي
al-farraa'ii
furrier

بائع السمك
baa'i' as-samak
fishmonger

بائع الدواجن
baa'i' ad-dawaajin
poultry shop

بائع العطور
baa'i' al-'uṭuur
perfumery

دكان معلبات
dukkaan mu'allabaat
delicatessen

السوق المركزية
as-suuq al-markaziyya
supermarket

كشك سجائر
kushik sajaa'ir
tobacconist

دكان آلات التصوير
dukkaan aalaat at-taṣwiir
camera shop

لوازم رياضية
lawaazim riyaaḍiyya
sporting goods

دكان الشراشف
dukkaan ash-sharaashif
household linen shop

محل اشرطة موسيقية
maḥall ashriṭa muusiqiyya
music shop (CDs, tapes, etc.)

لوازم منزلية
lawaazim manziliyah
household appliances (white goods)

دكان غسل ملابس
dukkaan ghasl malaabis
laundry

دكان مشتقات الحليب
dukkaan mushtaqqaat l-ḥaliib
dairy (shop selling dairy products)

صالون تجميل
ṣaaluun tajmiil
beauty salon

دكان ادوية الاعشاب
dukkaan adwiat al-a'shaab
herbalist's shop

صيدلية
ṣaydaliyya
pharmacy

بائع الورد
baa'i' al-ward
florist

خباز
khabbaaz
bakery

بائع الخضار
baai'i' al-khuḍar
greengrocer

دكان بوظة
dukkaan buuẓa
ice-cream shop

صائغ
ṣaa'igh
jeweler

المخزن الرئيسي
al-makhzan ar-ra'iissi
department store

مشتل
mashtal
nursery (plants)

10.1 Shopping conversations

Where can I get...?	أين أجد...؟
	ayna ajidu...?
When is this shop open?	متى يفتح هذا الدكان؟
	mataa yaftaḥu haadhaa ad-dukkaan?
Could you tell me where the...department is?	هل تدلني عن موقع قسم...؟
	hal tadullunii 'an mawqi'i qism al...?
Could you help me, please?	من فضلك، هل تساعدني على؟
	min faḍlik, hal tusaa'idunii 'alaa?

I'm looking for... _____ ... انا ابحث عن
anaa abhathu 'an...

Do you sell English / _____ هل تبيع صحف انكليزية/امريكية؟
American newspapers? hal tabii' suhuf inkiliiziyya / amariikiyya?

هل يوجد من يخدمك؟ _____ Are you being served?
hal yuujadu man yakhdimuka?

No, I'd like... _____ ... لا انا ارغب في
laa, anaa arghabu fii...

I'm just looking, if that's _____ انا ألقي نظرة فقط، هل في مانع
all right anaa ulqii nazra faqat, hal fii maani'

هل تطلب اي شيء اخر؟ _____ Would you like anything
hal tatlub ayya shay'in aakhar? else?

Yes, I'd also like... _____ ... نعم اريد ايضا
na'am, uriidu aydan...

No thank you, that's all _____ لا شكرا، هذا كل ما اريد
laa shukran, haadhaa kul maa uriid

Could you show me...? _____ هل تريني...؟
hal turiinii...?

I'd prefer... _____ ... أنا افضل
anaa ufaddil...

This is not what I'm looking _____ ليس هذا ما أريد
for laysa haadhaa maa uriid

Thank you, I'll keep looking _____ شكرا سأواصل البحث
shukran, sa-'uwaasil l-bahth

Do you have something...? _____ هل لديك بضاعة...؟
hal ladayka bidaa'atan'...?

- less expensive _____ أرخص
arkhas

- smaller _____ اصغر
asghar

- larger _____ اكبر
akbar

I'll take this one _____ سآخذ هذا
sa-'aakhudhu haadha

Does it come with instructions?	هل توجد تعليمات؟
	hal tuujadu ta'liimaat?

It's too expensive	غال جدا
	ghaalin jiddan

I'll give you...	سأعطيك...
	sa-u'tiika...

Could you keep this for me?	هل تحفظ هذا لي؟
	hal tahfaz haadha lii?

I'll come back for it later	سوف اعود فيما بعد
	sawfa a-'uud fiimaa ba'd

Do you have a bag for me, please?	هل لديك حقيبة لي من فضلك؟
	hal ladayka haqiiba lii min fadlik?

Could you gift-wrap it, please?	هل يمكن ان تغلفها لي من فضلك
	hal yumkin an tughallifahaa lii min fadlik?

انا اسف، ليس لدينا ذلك	I'm sorry, we don't have that
anaa aasif, laysa ladaynaa dhaalik	

آسف بعنا ما لدينا	I'm sorry, we're sold out
aasif bi'naa maa ladaynaa	

اسف لن تكون لدينا حتى	I'm sorry, it won't come back in until...
aasif lan takuuna ladaynaa hattaa...	

من فضلك، ادفع لدى امين الصندوق	Please pay at the cash register
min fadli, idfa' ladaa amiin as-sunduuq	

لا نقبل بطاقات الاعتماد	We don't accept credit cards
laa naqbal bataaqaat al-i'timaad	

لا نقبل شيك سياحي	We don't accept traveler's checks
laa naqbal shiik siyaahii	

لا نقبل عملات اجنبية	We don't accept foreign currency
laa naqbal 'umlaat ajnabiyya	

---

10 .2 Food

I'd like a hundred grams of..., please	اريد مئة غرام من...من فضلك
	uriidu mi'at ghraam min...min fadlik

I'd like half a kilo / five hundred grams of...	اريد نصف كيلو من...
	uriidu nisf kiilu min...

I'd like a kilo of... _____ اريد كيلوغرام من...
uriidu kiilughraaman min...

Could you...it for me, _____ هل يمكن ان...لي من فضلك
please? hal yumkin an...lii min fadlik?

- slice it / cut it up for me, ___ قطعها/اجعلها شرائح من فضلك
please qatt'ihaa / ij'alhaa sharaa'ih min fadlik

- grate it for me, please ____ قطعها الى قطع صغيرة، من فضلك
qatt'ihaa ilaa qita' saghiira min fadlik

Can I order it? _____ هل يمكن ان اطلب؟
hal yumkin an atluba?

I'll pick it up tomorrow / ____ سوف أخذه غدا/الساعة...
at... sawfa akhudhuhu ghadan / as-
sa'aa...

Can you eat / drink this? ____ هل يمكن ان تأكل/تشرب هذا؟
hal yumkin an ta'kula / tashraba
haadhaa?

What's in it? _____ ماذا فيه؟
maadhaa fiihi?

10 .3 Clothing and shoes

I saw something in the ____ رايت شيئا في الشباك
window ra'aytu shay'an fii ash-shubbaak

Shall I point it out? _____ هل يمكن ان اشير إلى ذلك؟
hal yumkin an ushiira ilaa dhaalika?

I'd like something to go ____ اريد شيئا يتناسب مع هذا
with this uriidu shay'an yatanaasab ma'a
haadha

Do you have shoes to ____ هل لديك حذاء يناسب هذا؟
match this? hal ladayka hidhaa' yunaasib haadha

I'm a size...in the USA ____ انا حجمي...في القياس الأمريكي
anaa hijmii...fii al-qiyaas al-amariikii

Can I try this on? _____ هل يمكن ان اجرب هذا؟
hal yumkin an ujarriba haadhaa?

Where's the fitting room? ____ اين غرفة القياس؟
ayna ghurfat al-qiyaas?

It doesn't suit me _____ انه لا يناسبني
innahu laa yunaasibunii

This is the right size _____ هذا هو الحجم المناسب
haadhaa huwa al-hajm al-munaasib

It doesn't look good on me — لا يبدو لائقا علي
laa yabduu laa'iqan 'alayya

Do you have this / these ____ هل لديك هذا / هذه في..؟
in...? hal ladayka haadhaa / haadhihi fii...?

The heel's too high / low ____ الكعب عال / منخفض جدا
al-ka'b 'aalin / munkhafid jiddan

Is this real leather? _____ هل هذا جلد حقيقي
hal haadha jild haqiiqii?

Is this genuine hide? _____ هل هذا جلد حيوان حقيقي
hal haadha jild hayawaan haqiiqii?

I'm looking for a...for a... ____ انا ابحث عن...لطفل عمره...
-year-old child anaa abhath 'an...litifl 'umruhu...

I'd like a... _____ اريد...
uriidu

- silk _____ حرير
hariir

- cotton _____ قطن
qutun

- woolen _____ صوفي
suufi

- linen _____ كتان
kittaan

At what temperature ____ ما هي درجة الحرارة المناسبة لغسله؟
should I wash it? maa hiya darajat al-haraara al-
munaasiba li-ghaslihi?

Will it shrink in the wash? ____ هل يتقلص عند الغسل؟
hal yataqallas 'inda al-ghasl?

لا تكوي	تنظيف جاف	غسل يدوي
laa takwii	tanziif jaaf	ghasl yadawi
Do not iron	Dry clean	Hand wash
إسط	لا تجفف بالدوران السريع	قابل للغسل بالغسالة
ibsit	laa tujaffif bid-dawaraan as-sarii'	qaabil lil-ghasl bil-ghassala
Lay flat	Do not spin dry	Machine washable

At the cobbler

Could you mend these ____ هل يمكن أن تصلح هذا الحذاء؟
shoes? hal yumkin an tusliha haadha al-
hidhaa'?

Shopping

Could you resole and _____ reheel these shoes?

هل يمكن أن تغير كعب هذا الحذاء؟
hal yumkin an tughayyira ka'b haadha l-hidhaa'?

When will they be ready? ____

متى تكون جاهزة؟
mataa takuun jaahiza?

I'd like..., please _____

اريد...من فضلك
uriidu...min fadlik

- a can of shoe polish _____

علبة معجون لتلميع الأحذية
'ulba ma'juun li-talmii' al-ahdhiya

- a pair of shoelaces _____

زوج من رباط الحذاء
zaw min ribaat al-hidhaa'

10.4 Photographs and video

I'd like a film for this _____ camera, please

اريد فلم لهذه الكاميرا من فضلك
uriidu film lihaadhihi al-kamiira min fadlik

I'd like a cartridge, please ___

اريد خرطوشة من فضلك
uriid khartuushat min fadlik

- a one twenty-six cartridge _

خرطوشة ذات ست وعشرون
khartuusha dhaat sit wa 'ishruun

- a slide film _____

فيلم إنزلاقي
film inzilaaqii

- a movie cassette, please ___

شريط فيلم من فضلك
shariit film min fadlik

- a videotape _____

شريط فيديو
shariit viidiyu

- color / black and white ____

ملون/اسود وابيض
mulawwan / aswad wa abyad

- super eight _____

علبة بثمانية
'ulba bi-thamaaniya

- 12 / 24 / 36 exposures ____

فلم ذو 12/24/36 صورة
film dhuu 12 / 24 / 36 suura

- ASA / DIN number _____

رقم اي اس اي/دي آي أن
raqm ay as ay / di aay an

Problems

Could you load the film for __ me, please?

هل تركب لي الفلم من فضلك؟
hal turakkib lii al-film min fadlik?

Could you take the film _____ out for me, please?

هل تخرج لي الفلم من فضلك؟
hal tukhrij lii al-film min fadlik?

Should I replace the _____ batteries?	هل يجب ان اغير البطاريات؟ hal yajibu an ughayyira al-battaariyyaat?
Could you have a look at ___ my camera, please?	هل تفحص الكامرا من فضلك؟ hal tafhas al-kamira min fadlik?
It's not working _____	انها لا تعمل innahaa laa ta'mal
The...is broken _____	الـ...مكسور al-...maksuur
The film's jammed _____	الفلم محشور al-film mahshuur
The film's broken _____	الفلم مكسور al-film maksuur
The flash isn't working _____	الضوء (الفلاش) لا يعمل ad-daw' (al-flash) laa ya'mal

Processing and prints

I'd like to have this film _____ developed and printed, please	من فضلك اريد ان اطبع هذا الفلم min fadlik uriidu an atba'a haadha al-film
I'd like...prints from each ____ negative	اريد...من كل صورة uriidu ...min kulli suura
- glossy / matte _____	لامع/ناعم laami'/ naa'im
- 6 x 9 _____	ستة في تسعة sitta fii tis'a
I'd like to order reprints of ___ these photos	اريد اعادة طبع هذه الصور uridu i'aadat tab' haadhihi as-suwar
I'd like to have this photo _____ enlarged	اريد تكبير هذه الصورة uriidu takbiir haadhihi as-suura
How much is processing? ___	كم سعر التحميض؟ kam si'r at-tahmid?
How much for printing? ____	كم سعر الطباعة؟ kam si'r at-tibaa'a?
How much are the reprints? _	كم سعر اعادة الطبع؟ kam si'r i'aadat at-tab'?
How much is it for _____ enlargement?	كم سعر التكبير؟ kam si'r at-takbiir?
When will they be ready? ____	متى تكون جاهزة؟ mataa takuun jaahiza?

Do I have to make an appointment? _____	هل من الضروري أن أحدد موعدا ؟ hal mina ad-daruurii an uhaddida maw'idan?
Can I come in right now? _____	هل استطيع ان ادخل الان؟ hal astatiu an adkhula al'aan?
How long will I have to wait? _____	هل انتظر طويلا ؟ hal antaziru tawiilan?
I'd like a shampoo / haircut _____	اريد شامبو/قصة شعر uriidu shaambuu / qassat sha'r
I'd like a shampoo for oily / dry hair, please _____	من فضلك اريد شامبو لشعر زيتي/جاف min fadlik uriidu shaambuu lisha'r zaytii / jaaf
I'd like an anti-dandruff shampoo _____	اريد شامبو ضد القشرة uriidu shaambuu did al-qishra
I'd like a color-rinse shampoo, please _____	اريد صبغة شامبو ملون من فضلك uriidu sibghat shaambuu mulawwin min fadlik
I'd like a shampoo with conditioner, please _____	اريد شامبو مع ملطف شعر من فضلك uriidu shaambuu ma'a mulattif sha'r min fadlik
I'd like highlights, please _____	اريد صبغ أطراف الشعر من فضلك uriidu sabgha atraaf ash-sha'r min fadlik
Do you have a color chart, please? _____	هل لديك خريطة الألوان، من فضلك ؟ hal ladayka khariita al-alwaan min fadlik?
I'd like to keep the same color _____	اريد ان احافظ على نفس اللون uriid an uhaafiza 'alaa nafs al-lawn
I'd like it darker / lighter _____	اريد لونا أغمق/أفتح uriidu lawnan aghmaq / aftah
I'd like / I don't want hairspray _____	أريد/لا أريد رشاش شعر uriidu / laa uriidu rashaash sha'r
- gel _____	جل jall
- lotion _____	مستحضر mustahdar
I'd like short bangs _____	أريد قصة قصيرة uriidu qassatan qasiiratan

Not too short at the back ____	ليس قصيرا من الخلف laysa qaṣiiran min al-khalf
Not too long ____	ليس طويلا جدا laysa tawiilan jiddan
I'd like it curly / not too ____ curly	أريده مجعدا/ليس مجعدا uriiduhu muja'-'adan / laysa muja'-'adan
It needs a little / a lot taken ____ off	يحتاج ان اقص منه قليلا/كثيرا yaḥtaaj an aquṣṣa minhu qaliilan / kathiiran
I'd like a completely ____ different style / a different cut	أريد تسريحة مختلفة تماما/قصة مختلفة uriidu tasriiḥa mukhtalifa tamaaman / qaṣṣatan mukhtalifatan
I'd like it the same as in ____ this photo	أريده كما في هذه الصورة uriiduhu kamaa fii haadhihi aṣ-ṣuura
- as that woman's ____	مثل تلك السيدة mithla tilka as-sayyida
Could you turn the drier ____ up / down a bit?	هل يمكن ان تخفف/تقوي المجفف قليلا؟ hal yumkin an tukhaffifa / tuqawwiya al-mujaffif qaliilan?
I'd like a facial ____	اريد تدليك الوجه uriidu tadliik al-wajh
- a manicure ____	صبغ أظافر اليد ṣabgh aẓaafir al-yad

كيف تريد أن أقصه لك؟ kayfa turiidu an aquṣṣahu laka? ____	How do you want it cut?
أية تسريحة تريد؟ ayyat tasriiḥa turiidu? ____	What style do you have in mind?
أي لون تريد؟ ayya lawnin turiidu? ____	What color do you want it?
هل درجة الحرارة مناسبة لك؟ hal darajat al-ḥaraara munaasiba laka? ____	Is the temperature all right for you?
هل ترغب في مطالعة بعض الصحف؟ hal targhab fii muṭaala'at ba'ḍ aṣ- ṣuḥuf? ____	Would you like something to read?
هل تريد مشروبا؟ hal turiidu mashruuban? ____	Would you like a drink?
هل هذا ما أردت؟ hal haadha maa aradta? ____	Is this what you had in mind?

| - a massage | تدليك |
| | tadliik |

| Could you give me a trim, please? | هل تخفف لي شعري من فضلك؟ |
| | hal tukhaffif lii sha'rii min fadlik? |

| - bangs | شعر ما فوق الجبين |
| | sha'r maa fawqa al-jabiin |

| - beard | لحية |
| | lihya |

| - moustache | شارب |
| | shaarib |

| I'd like a shave, please | أريد أن أحلق لحيتي من فضلك |
| | uriid an ahliqa lihyatii min fadlik |

| I'd like a wet shave, please | أريد حلاقة لحية مبللة من فضلك |
| | uriidu hilaaqat lihya muballala min fadlika |

At the Tourist Information Center

11 At the Tourist Information Center

11.1 Places of interest

• There are three main categories of tourist office: regional, provincial, and local. Regional offices are mainly concerned with planning and budgeting etc. Provincial offices usually have information on regions and towns. Tourist offices are generally open Saturday to Thursday 8.30a.m. to 12.30p.m. and 3.00p.m. to 6.30p.m.

Where's the Tourist Information, please?	لو سمحت اين مكتب الإستعلامات السياحية؟ law samahta, ayna maktabu al-ist'laamaat as-siyaahiya?
Do you have a city map?	هل لديك خارطة المدينة؟ hal ladayka khaaritat al-madiina?
Where is the museum?	اين المتحف؟ ayna al-mathaf?
Where can I find a church?	اين يمكن ان اجد كنيسة؟ ayna yumkin an ajida kaniisa?
Could you give me some information about...?	هل يمكن ان تزودني بمعلومات عن...؟ hal yumkin an tuzawwidanii bima'luumat 'an...?
How much is this?	كم سعر هذا؟ kam si'ru haadhaa?
What are the main places of interest?	ماهي المواقع المهمة؟ maa hiya al-mawaaqi' al-muhimma?
Could you point them out on the map?	هل يمكن ان تشير اليها على الخارطة من فضلك؟ hal yumkin an tushira ilayhaa 'alaa al-khaarita min fadlik?
What do you recommend?	بماذا تنصح؟ bi-maadhaa tansah?
We'll be here for a few hours	سنبقى هنا لبضعة ساعات sanabqaa hunaa li-bid'at saa'aat
We'll be here for a day	سنبقى هنا ليوم واحد sanabqaa hunaa li-yawmin waahid
We'll be here for a week	سنبقى هنا لمدة اسبوع sanabqaa hunaa li-muddat usbuu'
We're interested in...	نحن مهتمون بـ... nahnu muhtammun bi...

Is there a scenic walk around the city?	هل هناك طريق تنزه حول المدينة؟ hal hunaaka tariiqa tanazzuh hawla al-madiina?
How long does it take?	كم تستغرق؟ kam tastaghriq?
Where does it start / end?	اين تبدأ / تنتهي؟ ayna tabda'/ tantahii?
Are there any boat trips?	هل هناك اية رحلات بحرية؟ hal hunaaka ayyat rahalaat bahriyya?
Where can we board?	من أين نصعد الى المركب؟ min ayna nas'ad ilaa al-markab?
Are there any bus tours?	هل هناك اية رحلات بالباص؟ hal hunaaka ayyat rahalaat bil-baas?
Where do we get on?	من أين نركب؟ min ayna narkab?
Is there a guide who speaks English?	هل يوجد دليل سياحي يتكلم الانكيزية؟ hal yuujad daliil siyaahii yatakallam al-inkiliiziyya?
What trips can we take around the area?	اية رحلات يمكن ان نقوم بها حول هذه المنطقة؟ ayyat rahalaat yumkin an naquum bihaa hawla haadhihi al-mintaqa?
Are there any excursions?	هل هناك اية رحلات؟ hal hunaaka ayyat rahalaat?
Where do they go?	إلى اين يذهبون؟ ilaa ayna yadhhabuun?
How long is the excursion?	كم ستدوم الرحلة؟ kam sataduum ar-rihla?
How long do we stay in...?	كم سنبقى في...؟ kam sanabqaa fii...?
Are there any guided tours?	هل هناك اية رحلات يقودها دليل؟ hal hunaaka ayyat rahalaat yaquuduhaa daliil?
How much free time will we have there?	كم سنبقى هناك؟ kam sanabqaa hunaaka?
We want to have a walk around / to go on foot	نريد ان نتمشى في المنطقة / نريد ان نمشي على الأقدام nuriidu an natamashaa fii al-mintaqa / nuriidu an namshiya 'alaa al-aqdaam
Can we hire a guide?	هل يمكن ان نستعين بدليل؟ hal yumkin an nasta'iina bi-daliil?

11

What time does...open / close?	متى يفتح/يغلق الـ...؟ mataa yaftah / yughliq al...?
What days are...open / closed?	أي يوم يفتح/يغلق الـ...؟ ay yawm yaftah / yughliq al...?
What's the admission price?	ما هو رسم الدخول؟ maa huwa rasm ad-dukhuul?
Is there a group discount?	هل هناك تخفيض للمجموعات؟ hal hunaaka takhfiid lil-majmuu'aat?
Is there a child discount?	هل هناك تخفيض للاطفال؟ hal hunaaka takhfiid lil-atfaal?
Is there a discount for senior citizens?	هل هناك تخفيض للمسنين؟ hal hunaaka takhfiid lil-musiniin?
Can I take (flash) photos / can I film here?	هل استطيع ان آخذ صورا/هل يمكن ان اصور هنا؟ hal astatii'u an aakhudha suwaran / hal yumkin an usawwira hunaa?
Do you have any postcards of...?	هل لديك اية بطاقات بريدية لـ...؟ hal ladayka ayyat bitaaqaat bariidiyya...?
Do you have an English...?	هل لديك...باللغة الانكليزية؟ hal ladayka...bil-lugha al-inkiliiziyya?
- catalogue	كتالوغ kataaluugh
- program	برنامج barnaamaj
- brochure	كراسة نماذج kurraasat namaadhij

11.2 Going out

• Going out for artistic and cultural events depends very much on the specific city and country you are visiting. Generally speaking, most of the festivals, cultural events and concerts are organized during summer.

Do you have this week's / month's entertainment guide?	هل لديك دليل البرامج الترفيهية لهذة الليلة/لهذا الشهر؟ hal ladayka daliil al-baraamij at-tarfiihiya lihaadhihi al-layla / lihaadha ash-shahr?
What's on tonight?	ماذا يوجد هذه الليلة؟ maadhaa yuujad haadhihi al-layla?

We want to go to... _____ نريد ان نذهب الى...
nuriidu an nadhhaba ilaa...

What's playing at the _____ أي فيلم يبث في السينما ؟
cinema? ay film yubath fii as-siinimaa?

What sort of film is that? ____ اي نوع من الافلام هذا ؟
ay naw'in min al-aflaam haadha?

- suitable for everyone _____ يناسب الجميع
yunaasib al-jamii'

- not suitable for people_____ لا يناسب الأشخاص دون سن الثانية
under 12 / under 16 عشرة/السادسة عشرة
laa yunaasib al-ashkhaas duuna sin
ath-thaaniya 'ashara / as-saadisa
'ashara

- original version _____ النسخة الاصلية
an-nuskha al-asliyya

- subtitled _____ معنون
mu'anwan

- dubbed _____ مدبلج
mudablaj

Is it a continuous showing? __ هل هذا عرض مستمر ؟
hal haadhaa 'ard mustamir?

What's on at...? _____ ماذا يقدم في...؟
maadhaa yuqaddam fii...?

- the theater _____ المسرح
al-masrah

- the opera _____ الاوبرا
al-uubiraa

What's happening in the ____ ما هو برنامج قاعة الموسيقي ؟
concert hall? maa huwa barnaamaj qaa'at al-
muusiiqa?

Where can I find a good ____ اين يمكن ان اجد ديسكو جيد هنا ؟
disco around here? ayna yumkin an ajidaa diisku jayyid
hunaa?

Is it members only? _____ هل هذا خاص بالأعضاء المنتسبين فقط ؟
hal haadhaa khaas bil-a'daa' al-
muntasibiin faqat?

Where can I find a good ____ اين يمكن ان اجد نادي ليلي جيد هنا ؟
nightclub around here? ayna yumkin an ajidaa naadii laylii
jayyid hunaa?

Is it evening wear only? _____	هل يجب أن أرتدي لباسا خاصا بالحفلات المسائية؟
	hal yajibu an artadiya libaasan khaasan bil-hafalaat al-masaa'iyya?

Should I (we) dress up? _____	هل يجب ان البس (نلبس) لباسا رسميا ؟
	hal yajibu an albasa (nalbasa) libaasan rasmiyyan?

What time does the show start? _____	متى يبدأ العرض؟
	mataa yabda'u al-'ard?

When's the next soccer match? _____	ما موعد مباراة كرة القدم القادمة؟
	maa maw'id mubaaraat kurat al-qadam al-qaadima?

Who's playing? _____	من الذي يلعب؟
	man alladhii yal'ab?

I'd like an escort for tonight _____	اريد مرافقا لهذه الليلة
	uriidu muraafiqan li-haadhihi al-layla

11 .3 Reserving tickets

Could you reserve some tickets for us? _____	هل يمكن ان تحجز لنا بعض التذاكر من فضلك؟
	hal yumkin an tahjiza lanaa ba'd at-tadhaakir min fadlik?

We'd like to book...seats / a table for... _____	نريد ان نحجز...مقاعد/طاولة لـ...
	nuriidu an nahjiza...maqaa'id / taawila li...

- seats in the orchestra in the main section _____	مقاعد في الاركسترا في القسم الرئيسي
	maqaa'id fii al-urkistraa fii al-qism ar-ra'iisii

- seats in the circle _____	مقاعد في الدائرة
	maqaa'id fii ad-daa'ira

- a box for... _____	ركنا لـ...
	ruknan li...

- front row seats / a table for...at the front _____	مقاعد في الصف الامامي/طاولة لـ... في الامام
	maqaa'id fii as-saf al-amaamii / taawila li...fii al-amaam

- seats in the middle / a table in the middle _____	مقاعد في الوسط/طاولة في الوسط
	maqaa'id fii al-wasat / taawila fii al-wasat

- back row seats / a table at the back _____	مقاعد في الصف الخلفي/طاولة في الخلف
	maqaa'id fii as-saf al-khalfii / taawila fii as-saf al-khalfi

Could I reserve...seats for the...o'clock performance? ___

هل يمكن ان احجز...مقاعد لعرض الساعة...؟

hal yumkin an ahjiza...maqaa'id li'ard as-saa'a...?

Are there any seats left for tonight? ___

هل توجد اية تذاكر متبقية لهذه الليلة؟

hal tuujad ayyat tadhaakir mutabaqiya lihaadhihi al-layla?

How much is a ticket? ___

كم سعر التذكرة؟

kam si'r at-tadhkira

When can I pick up the tickets? ___

متى يمكن ان استلم التذاكر؟

mataa yumkin an astalima at-tadhaakir?

I've got a reservation ___

لدي حجز

ladayya hajz

My name's... ___

اسمي...

ismii...

تريد ان تحجز لأي عرض؟ ___

turiid an tahjiza li-ayya 'ardin?

Which performance do you want to reserve for?

اين تريد ان تجلس؟ ___

ayna turiidu an tajlisa?

Where would you like to sit?

بيع كل شيء ___

bii'a kulu shay'in

Everything's sold out

غرفة للوقوف فقط ___

ghurfa lil-wuquuf faqat

It's standing room only

لدينا مقاعد دائرية فقط ___

ladaynaa maqaa'ida daa'iriyya faqat

We've only got circle seats left

لدينا مقاعد دائرية عليا فقط ___

ladaynaa maqaa'ida daa'iriyya 'ulyaa faqat

We've only got upper circle (way upstairs) seats left

لدينا مقاعد للفرقة الموسيقية فقط ___

ladaynaa maqaa'id lil-firqa al-muusiiqiyya faqat

We've only got orchestra seats left

هناك مقاعد في الصف الامامي ___

hunaaka maqaa'id fii as-saf al-amaamii

We've only got front row seats left

هناك مقاعد في المؤخرة ___

hunaaka maqaa'id fii al-mu'akhara

We've only got seats left at the back

كم مقعدا تريد؟ ___

kam maq'adan turiidu?

How many seats would you like?

— يجب اب تستلم التذاكر قبل الساعة...   You'll have to pick up the
yajib an tastalima at-ta<u>dh</u>aakir qabla   tickets before...o'clock
  as-saa'a...

التذاكر من فضلك _____ Tickets, please
at-ta<u>dh</u>aakir min fa<u>d</u>lik

هذا مقعدك _____ This is your seat
haa<u>dh</u>aa maq'aduk

أنت في المقعد الخطأ _____ You are in the wrong seat
anta fii al-maq'ad al-<u>kh</u>a<u>t</u>a'

Sports

12 **S**ports

12.1 **S**porting questions

| Where can we...around here? | اين يمكن ان...هنا ؟ |
| | ayna yumkin an...hunaa? |

Can we hire a...?
هل يمكنني ان استأجر...؟
hal yumkinuni an asta'jira...?

Can we take lessons?
هل يمكن ان نتلقى دروسا ؟
hal yumkin an natalaqaa duruusan?

For beginners / intermediates
للمبتدئين/للمتوسطين
lil-mubtadi'iin / al-mutawassitiin

How large are the groups?
ما حجم للمجموعات؟
maa hajm al-majmuu'aat?

What languages are the classes in?
بأية لغة تعطى للدروس ؟
bi-ayyati lugha tu'taa ad-duruus?

How much is that per hour / per day?
كم الاجرة في الساعة/اليوم؟
kam al-ujra fii as-saa'a / al-yawm?

How much is each one?
كم سعر الواحد ؟
kam si'r al-waahid?

Do you need a permit for that?
هل تحتاج الى رخصة لهذا ؟
hal tahtaaj ilaa rukhsa li-haadhaa?

Where can I get the permit?
من اين يمكن الحصول على رخصة ؟
min ayna yumkin al-husuul 'alaa rukhsa?

12.2 **B**y the waterfront

Is it far to walk to the sea?
هل يمكن أن أذهب الى البحر مشيا ؟
hal yumkin an adhhaba ilaa al-bahri mashyan?

Is there a...around here?
هل يوجد...هنا ؟
hal yuujad...huna?

- a swimming pool
مسبح
masbah

- a sandy beach
شاطئ رملي
shaati' ramlii

- a nudist beach
شاطئ للعراة
shaati' lil-'uraat

- a mooring place / dock
رصيف/مرسى
marsaa / rasiif

Sports

Are there any rocks here? _____	هل توجد أي صخور هنا ؟ hal tuujad ay sukhuur hunaa?
When's high / low tide? _____	متى يكون أعلى/اقل مستوى للمد ؟ mataa yakuun a'laa / aqal mustawaa lil-mad?
What's the water _____ temperature?	ما هي درجة حرارة الماء ؟ maa hiya darajat haraarat al-maa'?
Is it very deep here? _____	هل هذا عميق جدا ؟ hal haadha 'amiiq jiddan?
Is it safe for children to _____ swim here?	هل يمكن للاطفال ان يسبحوا هنا بأمان ؟ hal yumkin lil-atfaal an yasbahuu hunaa bi-amaan?
Are there any currents? _____	هل توجد تيارات ؟ hal tuujad tayyaaraat?
Are there any rapids along _ this river?	هل توجد اية منحدرات او شلالات في هذا النهر ؟ hal tuujad ayyat munhadaraat aw shallaalaat fii haadhaa an-nahr?
What does that flag / buoy _____ mean?	ماذا يعني ذلك العلم/العوامة ؟ maadhaa ya'nii dhaalika al-'alam / al-'awwaama?
Is there a lifeguard on _____ duty?	هل يوجد رجل انقاذ ؟ hal yuujad rajul inqaadh?
Are dogs allowed here? _____	هل مسموح بالكلاب هنا ؟ hal masmuuh bil-kilaab hunaa?
Is camping on the beach _____ allowed?	هل يسمح بنصب الخيام في هذا الشاطيء ؟ hal yusmah bi-nasbi al-khiyaam fii haadhaa ash-shaati'?
Can we light a fire? _____	هل يمكن ان نشعل النار ؟ hal yumkin an nush'ila an-naar?

Sports

12

مياه الصيد miyaah as-sayd Fishing waters	برخصة فقط birukhsa faqat Permits only	ممنوع التزلج الشراعي mamnuu' at-tazalluj ash-shiraa'ii No surfing
خطر khatar Danger	ممنوع السباحة mamnuu' as-sibaaha No swimming	ممنوع الصيد mamnuu' as-sayd No fishing

Sickness

13 Sickness

13.1 Call (get) the doctor

• If you become ill or need emergency treatment, it is best to go to Casualty (*istijalii*) at your nearest hospital.

Could you call a doctor _____ quickly, please?	هل يمكن ان تتصل بطبيب بسرعة من فضلك؟ hal yumkin an tattasil bitabiib bisur'a min fadlik?
When does the doctor _____ have office hours?	ماهي ساعات عمل الطبيب؟ maa hiya saa'aat 'amal at-tabiib?
When can the doctor _____ come?	متى يأتي الطبيب؟ mataa ya'tii at-tabiib?
Could I make an _____ appointment to see the doctor?	هل يمكن ان أحدد موعدا لزيارة الطبيب؟ hal yumkin an uhaddida maw'idan liziyaarat at-tabiib?
I've got an appointment to _ see the doctor at...o'clock	لدي موعد مع الطبيب على الساعة... ladayya maw'id ma'a at-tabiib 'alaa sa-saa'a...
Which doctor / pharmacy _____ is on night / weekend duty?	أي طبيب/صيدلية مفتوح ليلا/خلال عطلة نهاية الاسبوع؟ ay tabiib / saydaliyya maftuuh laylan / khilaal 'utlat nihaayat al-usbuu'?

13.2 Patient's ailments

I don't feel well _____	اشعر بالم ash'uru bi-'alam
I'm dizzy _____	اشعر بدوار ash'uru bi-duwaar
- ill _____	مريض mariid
I feel sick (nauseous) _____	اشعر برغبة في التقيؤ ash'uru bi-raghba fii at-taqayyu'
I've got a cold _____	عندي زكام 'indii zukaam
It hurts here _____	الالم هنا al-alam hunaa
I've been sick (vomited) _____	كنت اتقيأ kuntu ataqayya'

| I've got... _____ | أشعر بـ../عندي |
| | 'indii / ash'uru bi |

| I'm running a temperature of...degrees _____ | حرارتي هي...درجات |
| | haraaratii hiya...darajaat |

| I've been... _____ | كنت ... |
| | kuntu... |

| - stung by a wasp _____ | لدغتني نحلة |
| | ladaghatnii nahlaa |

| - stung by an insect _____ | لدغتني حشرة |
| | ladaghatnii hashara |

| - bitten by a dog _____ | عضني كلب |
| | 'addanii kalb |

| - stung by a jellyfish _____ | لدغتني قنديل البحر |
| | ladaghanii qandiil al-bahr |

| - bitten by a snake _____ | لدغتني حية |
| | ladaghatnii hayya |

| - bitten by an animal _____ | عضني حيوان |
| | 'addanii hayawaan |

| I've cut myself _____ | جرحت نفسي |
| | jarahtu nafsii |

| I've burned myself _____ | حرقت نفسي |
| | haraqtu nafsii |

| I've grazed / scratched myself _____ | خدشت/حككت نفسي |
| | khadashtu / hakaktu nafsii |

| I've had a fall _____ | وقعت على الارض |
| | waqa'tu 'alaa al-ard |

| I've sprained my ankle _____ | التوى كاحلي/كعبي |
| | iltawaa kahilii / ka'ibii |

| I'd like the morning-after pill _____ | افضل حبوب منع الحمل الصباحية |
| | ufadilu hubuub mani' al-haml as-sabaahiya |

Sickness

13

13.3 The consultation

| ما المشلكة؟ _____ | What seems to be the problem? |
| maa l-mushkila? | |

| منذ متى تشكو من هذا _____ | How long have you had these complaints? |
| mundhu mataa tashkuu min haadha? | |

هل حصلت لديك هذه المشكلة من قبل؟	hal hasalat ladayka haadhihi al-mushkila min qabl	— Have you had this trouble before?
هل تعرف درجة حرارتك؟ ماهي؟	hal ta'rif darajat haraaratik? maa hiya?	—— Do you have a temperature? What is it?
اخلع (انزع) ثيابك من فضلك	ikhla' (inza') thiyaabaka min fadlik	—— Get undressed, please
انزع الى حد الخصر من فضلك	inza' ilaa haddi l-khisr min fadlik	—— Strip to the waist, please
يمكن ان تنزع ثيابك هناك	yumkin an tanzi'a thiyaabaka hunaa	——— You can undress there
اكشف عن ذراعك الايمان/الايسر من فضلك	ikshif 'an dhiraa'ika al-ayman / al-aysar min fadlik	— Roll up your left / right sleeve, please
استلق هنا من فضلك	istalqii hunaa min fadlik	—— Lie down here, please
هل هذا يؤلمك؟	hal haadhaa yu'limuk?	——— Does this hurt?
خذ نفسا عميقا	khudh nafsa 'amiiq	—— Breathe deeply
افتح فمك	iftah famak	—— Open your mouth

Patients' medical history

I'm a diabetic	عندي السكري	'indii as-sukkarii
I have a heart condition	اعاني من مرض القلب	u'aanii min marad al-qalb
I'm asthmatic	اعاني من الربو	u'aanii min ar-rabuu
I'm allergic to...	لدي حساسية ضد...	ladayya hassaasiyya didda...
I'm...months pregnant	انا حامل في الشهر...	anaa haamil fii ash-shahr...
I'm on a diet	لدي نظام غذائي	ladayya nizaam ghidhaa'ii
I'm on medication / the pill	أتابع علاجا/أتناول حبوبا	utaabi'u 'ilaajan / atanaawalu hubuuban

I've had a heart attack once before	تعرضت لازمة قلبية مرة واحدة في السابق ta'arradtu li'azma qalbiyya marratan waahida fii as-sabiq
I've had an operation on my...	أجريت على عملية جراحية في... ujriyat 'alayya 'amaliyya jirahiyya fii...
I've been ill recently	أصبحت مريضا منذ وقت قصير asbahtu mariidan mundhu waqtin qasiirin
I've got a stomach ulcer	عندي قرح في المعدة 'indii qurh fii al-ma'ida
I've got my period	انا في الدورة الشهرية anaa fii ad-dawra ash-shahriyya

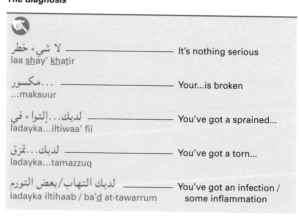

هل لديك اية حساسية؟ hal ladayka ayyat hassaasiyya?	Do you have any allergies?
هل تتابع اي علاج حاليا؟ hal tutaabi' ay 'ilaaj haaliyyan?	Are you on any medication?
هل لديك نظام غذائي؟ hal ladayka nizaam ghidhaa'ii?	Are you on a diet?
هل انت حامل؟ hal anti haamil?	Are you pregnant?
هل سبق ان اخذت حقنة ضد الكزاز؟ hal sabaqa an akhadhta hukna did al-kuzaaz?	Have you had a tetanus injection?

The diagnosis

لا شيء خطر laa shay' khatir	It's nothing serious
...مكسور ...maksuur	Your...is broken
لديك...إلتواء في ladayka...iltiwaa' fii	You've got a sprained...
لديك...تمزق ladayka...tamazzuq	You've got a torn...
لديك التهاب/بعض التورم ladayka iltihaab / ba'd at-tawarrum	You've got an infection / some inflammation

لديك التهاب الزائدة _____ You've got appendicitis
ladayka iltihaab az-zaa'ida

لديك التهاب رئوي _____ You've got bronchitis
ladayka iltihaab ri'awii

لديك مرض تناسلي _____ You've got a venereal
ladayka marad tanaasulii   disease

انت مصاب بالانفلونزا _____ You've got the flu
anta musaab bil-influwanza

تعرضت لازمة قلبية _____ You've had a heart attack
ta'arradta li-'azma qalbiyya

لديك التهاب بكتيري/فيروسي _____ You've got a (viral /
ladayka iltihaab baktiirii / fiiruusi   bacterial) infection

لديك التهاب رئوي حاد _____ You've got pneumonia
ladayka iltihaab ri'awii haad

لديك التهاب/قرح في المعدة _____ You've got gastritis / an
ladayka iltihaab / qurh fii al-ma'ida   ulcer

لديك تمطط عضلي _____ You've pulled a muscle
lakayka tamattut 'adalii

لديك التهاب في المهبل _____ You've got a vaginal
ladayki iltihaab fii al-mahbal   infection

أصبت بتسمم غذائي _____ You've got food poisoning
usibta bi-tasammum ghidhaa'ii

أصبت بضربة شمس _____ You've got sunstroke
usibta bi-darbat shams

لديك حساسية ضد... _____ You're allergic to...
ladayka hassasiyya didda...

انت حامل _____ You're pregnant
anti haamil

اريد تحليل دمك/بولك/برازك _____ I'd like to have your blood /
uriidu tahliil damak / bawlak /   urine / stools tested
   biraazak

هذا يحتاج الى تغريز _____ It needs stitches
haadhaa yahtaaj ilaa taghriiz

احيلك الى طبيب اخصائي/ارسلك _____ I'm referring you to a
   الى المستشفى   specialist / sending you to
uhiiluka ilaa tabiib akhissaa'ii /   the hospital
   ursiluka ilaa al-mustashfaa

انت تحتاج الى فحص اشعة أكس _____ You'll need some X-rays
anta tahtaaj ilaa fahis ashi'at akis   taken

133

— Could you wait in the waiting room, please?

هل يمكن ان تنتظر في قاعة الانتظار من فضلك؟

hal yumkin an tantazir fii qaa'at al-intizaar min fadlik?

_____ You'll need an operation

انت تحتاج الى عملية جراحية

anta tahtaaj ilaa 'amaliyya jiraahiyya

Is it contagious? _____	هل هذا مرض معدي؟
	hal haadhaa marad mu'dii?
How long do I have to _____ stay...?	كم يجب ان ابقى...؟
	kam yajib an abqaa...?
- in bed _____	في الفراش
	fii al-firaash
- in the hospital _____	في المستشفى
	fii al-mustashfaa
Do I have to go on a special _____ diet?	هل يجب ان اتابع نظاما غذائيا خاصا؟
	hal yajib an utaabi'a nizaaman ghidhaa'iian khaasan
Am I allowed to travel? _____	هل مسموح لي بالسفر؟
	hal masmuhun lii bis-safar?
Can I make another _____ appointment?	هل يمكن ان أحدد موعدا اخر؟
	hal yumkin an uhaddida maw'idan aakhar?
When do I have to come _____ back?	ما هو موعد الفحص القادم؟
	maa huwa maw'id al-fahis al-qaadim?
I'll come back tomorrow _____	سوف آتي غدا
	sawfa aatii ghadan
How do I take this _____ medicine?	كيف آخذ هذا الدواء؟
	kayfa aakhudhu haadhaa d-dawaa'?

_____ Come back tomorrow / in...days' time

تعال غدا / خلال...ايام

ta'aala ghadan / khilaal...ayyaam

13.4 Medication and prescriptions

How many pills / drops / _____ injections / spoonfuls / tablets each time?	كم كبسولة / قطرة / حقنة / ملعقة / حبة في كل مرة؟
	kam kabsuula / qatara / huqna / mil'aqa / habba fii kul marra?

Sickness

13

How many times a day? _____ كم مرة في اليوم؟
kam marra fii al-yawm?

I've forgotten my _____ نسيت الدواء
medication
nasiitu ad-dawaa'

At home I take... _____ في البيت آخذ...
fii al-bayt aakhudhu...

Could you write a _____ هل يمكن ان تكتبا لي وصفة من فضلك؟
prescription for me, please?
hal yumkin an taktuba lii wasfa min
fadlik?

كتبت لك مضاد حيوي/خليط/مهدي ء/ _ I'm prescribing antibiotics/
مسكن الالم
a mixture / a tranquillizer/
pain killers
katabtu laka mudaad hayawii/khaliit/
muhaddi' / musakkin al-alam

عليك بالراحة _____ Have lots of rest
'alayka bi-rraaha

إبق في البيت _____ Stay indoors
ibqaa fii al-bayt

لازم الفراش _____ Stay in bed
laazim al-firaash

قبل الوجبات	حل (ذوب) في الماء	كبسول
qabla al-wajbaat	hil (dhawwib) fii	kabsuul
before meals	al-maa'	pills
	dissolve in water	
هذا العلاج يؤثر على السياقة	قطرات	حبوب
haadha al-'ilaaj	qatraat	hubuub
yu'athir 'laa as-siyaaqa	drops	tablets
this medication impairs your driving	ابلع	أكمل الوصفة
	ibla'	akmil al-wasfa
استعمال خارجي فقط	swallow (whole)	finish the prescription
isti'maal khaarijii faqat	كل...ساعات	ملعقة/ملعقة شاي
external use only	kul...saa'aat	mal'aqat / mal'aqat shaay
دلك	every...hours	spoonful / teaspoonful
dalk	مرهم	حقنات
rub on	marham	huqnaat
مرات في اليوم	ointment	injections
...marraat fii al-yawm	خذ	لمدة...ايام
...times a day	khud	limuddat...ayyaam
	take	for...days

13.5 At the dentist's

Do you know a good _____ dentist?	هل تعرف طبيب اسنان جيد ؟ hal ta'rif ṭabiib asnaan jayyid?
Could you make a dentist's _____ appointment for me?	هل يمكن ان تحدد لي موعدا مع طبيب اسنان؟ hal yumkin an tuḥaddida lii maw'idan ma'a ṭabiib al-asnan?
It's urgent _____	مستعجل musta'jal
Can I come in today, please? _____	هل استطيع ان أتي اليوم ؟ hal astaṭii' an aa-tiya al-yawm?
I have a terrible toothache _____	أعاني من الم شديد في الاسنان u'aanii min alam shadiid fii al-asnaan
Could you prescribe / give _____ me a painkiller?	هل يمكن أن تصف لي/تعطيني مسكن للالم؟ hal yumkin an taṣifa lii / tu'ṭiyanii musakkin lil-alam?
I've got a broken tooth _____	لدي سن مكسور ladayya sinn maksuur
My filling's come out _____	سقطت الحشوة saqaṭat al-ḥashwa
I've got a broken crown _____	لدي كسر في تاج السن ladayya kasr fii taaj as-sinn
I'd like / I don't want a local _____ anesthetic	اريد/لا اريد تخدير موضعي uriidu / laa uriidu takhdiir mawḍi'ii
Could you do a temporary _____ repair?	هل يمكن ان تصلحه مؤقتا ؟ hal yumkin an uṣliḥahu mu'aqqatan?
I don't want this tooth _____ pulled	لا اريد قلع هذا السن laa uridu qal'a haadhaa as-sinn
My denture is broken _____	فكي الاصطناعي مكسور fakkii al-iṣtinaa'ii maksur
Can you fix it? _____	هل يمكن ان تصلحه ؟ hal yumkin an tuṣliḥahu?

اي سن يؤلمك؟ ay sinn yu'limuka?	Which tooth hurts?
لديك صديد ladayka ṣadiid	You've got an abscess
يجب ان أفحص قناة جذر السن yajibu an afḥaṣa qanat jadhr as-sinn	I'll have to do a root canal

ساعطيك تخدير موضعي _____ — I'm giving you a local
sa'uutiika takhdiir mawdi'ii anesthetic

يجب ان اقلع/احشي/ابرد هذا السن — I'll have to pull / fill / file this
yajibu an aqla'a / ahshiya / abruda tooth
haadhaa as-sinn

يجب ان أحفره _____ — I'll have to drill it
yajibu an ahfirahu

افتح فمك من فضلك _____ — Open wide, please
iftah famaka min fadlik

اغلق من فضلك _____ — Close your mouth, please
aghliq min fadlik

اغسل من فضلك _____ — Rinse, please
ighsil min fadlik

هل ما زال يؤلمك؟ _____ — Does it hurt still?
hal maazaala yu'limuka?

In trouble

14 In trouble

14.1 Asking for help

Help! _____	النجدة an-najda!
Fire! _____	حريق/نار ḥariiq/naar!
Police! _____	يا بوليس (شرطة) yaa buuliis (shurṭa)!
Quick / Hurry! _____	عجل/بسرعه 'ajjil / bisur'a!
Danger! _____	خطر khaṭar!
Watch out! _____	احذر iḥdhar!
Stop! _____	قف qif!
Be careful! / Go easy! _____	إحذر (انتبه)/تمهل iḥdhar (intabih) / tamahhal!
Get your hands off me! ____	ارفع يدك عني irfa' yadaka 'annii!
Let go! _____	أتركني utruknii!
Stop thief! _____	اوقف اللص awqif al-liṣ!
Could you help me, please? _	هل يمكن ان تساعدني من فضلك؟ hal yumkin an tusaa'idanii min faḍlik?
Where's the police station / emergency exit / fire escape?	أين مركز الشرطة/مخرج الطواري ء/مهرب الحريق؟ ayna markaz ash-shurṭa / makhraj aṭ-ṭawaari' / mahrab al-ḥariiq?
Where's the nearest fire extinguisher?	أين اجد اقرب قنينة اطفاء الحريق؟ ayna ajid aqrab qanninat iṭfaa' al-ḥariiq?
Call the fire department! ___	أطلب رجال المطافي ء uṭlub rijaal al-maṭafi'!
Call the police! _____	اطلب (اتصل بـ) الشرطة uṭlub (ittaṣil bi) ash-shurṭa!
Call an ambulance! _____	اطلب (اتصل بـ) سيارة الاسعاف uṭlub (ittaṣil bi) sayyaarat al-is'aaf!

Where's the nearest phone? _ اين اجد اقرب هاتف؟
ayna ajidu aqraba haatif?

Could I use your phone? ____ هل يمكن ان استخدم هاتفك؟
hal yumkin an astakhdima haatifaka

What's the emergency ____ ما هو رقم هاتف الطوارىء؟
number? maa huwa raqm haatif at-tawaari'?

What's the number for the __ ما رقم هاتف الشرطة؟
police? maa raqm haatif ash-shurta?

14.2 Loss

I've lost my wallet _____ فقدت محفظتي
faqadtu mihfazatii

I lost my...here yesterday ____ فقدت...هنا امس
faqadtu...hunaa amsi

I left my...here _____ تركت...هنا
taraktu...hunaa

Did you find my...? _____ هل وجدت...؟
hal wajadta...?

It was right here _____ كانت هنا
kaanat hunaa

It's very valuable _____ انه ثمين جدا
innahu thamiin jiddan

Where's the lost and found __ اين دائرة البحث عن المفقودات؟
office? ayna daa'irat al-bahthi 'an al-
mafquudaat

14.3 Accidents

There's been an accident ____ وقع حادث
waqa'a haadith

Someone's fallen into the __ سقط شخص في الماء
water saqata shakhsun fii l-maa'

There's a fire _____ هناك حريق
hunaaka hariiq

Is anyone hurt? _____ هل تعرض اي شخص للأذى؟
hal ta'arrada ayya shakhsin lil-adhaa?

Nobody / someone has ____ لا أحد/شخص ماجرح
been injured laa ahada / shakhsun maa juriha

Someone's still trapped _____ inside the car / train	مازال شخص ما محبوس داخل السيارة/ القطار maa zaala shakhsun maa mahbuusun daakhila as-sayyaara / al-qitaar
It's not too bad _____	الحالة ليست سيئة جدا al-haala laysat sayyi'a jiddan
Don't worry _____	لا تقلق laa taqlaq
Leave everything the way _____ it is, please	اترك كل شيء كما هو من فضلك utruk kulla shay'in kamma huwa, min fadlik
I want to talk to the police _____ first	اريد ان اتحدث الى الشرطة اولا uriidu an atahaddatha ila ash-shurta awwalan
I want to take a photo first _____	اريد ان ألتقط صورة اولا uriidu an altaqita suuratan awwalan
Here's my name and _____ address	هذا اسمي وعنواني haadhaa ismii wa 'unwaanii
May I have your name _____ and address?	الإسم و العنوان لو سمحت؟ al-'ism wa al-'unwaan law samahta
Could I see your identity _____ card / your insurance papers?	من فضلك بطاقتك الشخصية/اوراق التأمين؟ min fadlik bitaaqatuka ash-shakhsiyya / awraaq at-ta'miin?
Will you act as a witness? _____	هل يمكن ان تدلي بشهادة؟ hal yumkin an tadliya bi-shahaada?
I need this information for _____ insurance purposes	احتاج لهذه المعلومات لأغراض التأمين ahtaaju li-haadhihi al-ma'luumaat li-'aghraad at-ta'miin
Are you insured? _____	هل أنت مؤمن؟ hal anta mu'amman?
Third party or all inclusive? _____	تأمين جزئي أم شامل؟ ta'miin juz'ii am shaamil?
Could you sign here, _____ please?	هل يمكن ان توقع هنا من فضلك؟ hal yumkin an tuwaqqi'a hunaa min fadlika?

14.4 Theft

I've been robbed _____	تعرضت للسرقة ta'arradtu lis-sariqa

My...has been stolen _____	...سرق مني ...suriqa minnii
My car's been broken into ___	سيارتي خلعت sayyaratii khuli'at

14.5 Missing person

I've lost my child / grandmother _____	فقدت طفلي/جدتي faqadtu tiflii / jaddatii
Could you help me find _____ him / her?	هل تساعدني في البحث عنه/عنها ؟ hal tusaa'idunii fii al-bahthi 'anhu / 'anhaa?
Have you seen a small _____ child?	هل رأيت طفلا صغيرا ؟ hal ra'ayta tifl saghiir?
She's / he's...years old _____	عمرها/عمره...سنة 'umruhaa / 'umruhu...sana
He's / she's got...hair _____	شعره/شعرها...اللون sha'ruhu / sha'ruhaa...al-lawn
- short / long _____	طويل/قصير tawiil / qasiir
- blond / red / brown / _____ black / gray	اشقر/احمر/بني/اسود/رمادي ashqar / ahmar / bunnii / aswad / ramaadii
- curly / straight / frizzy _____	مجعد/مسبل/مجعد muja'ad / musbal / muja'ad
- in a ponytail _____	تسريحة ذيل الحصان tasriihat dhayl al-hisaan
- in braids _____	ضفائر dafaa'ir
- in a bun _____	تسريحة tasriiha
He's / she's got blue / _____ brown / green eyes	عيناه/عيناها خضراوان/زرقاوان/بنيتان 'aynaah / 'aynaahaa khadraawaan / zarqaawaan / buniyyataan
He / she's wearing... _____	هو يلبس/هي تلبس... huwa yalbas / hiya talbas ...
- swimming trunks / _____ hiking boots	تبان سباحة/حذاء تسلق الجبال tubbaan sibaha / hidhaa' tasalluq al-jibaal
- with / without glasses _____	لابس/بدون نظارات laabis / biduun nazzaraat

- carrying / not carrying a bag	يحمل/لا يحمل حقيبة yahmil / laa yahmil haqiiba
He / She is short	هوقصير/هي قصيرة huwa qasiir / hiya qasiira
This is a photo of him / her	هذه صورته/صورتها haadhihi suuratuhu / suuratuhaa
He / She must be lost	انه لا بد ان تكون مفقودة innahu / innahaa laa budda an takuun mafquuda
She must be lost	انها لا بد ان تكون مفقودة innahaa laa budda an takuun mafquuda

14.6 The police

An arrest

Your (vehicle) documents, please	وثائقك (اوراق) سيارتك من فضلك wathaa'iq (awraaq) sayyaaratik min fadlik
You were speeding	كنت تسوق بسرعة kunta tasuuq bisur'at
You're not allowed to park here	لا يسمح لك بايقاف سيارتك هنا laa yusmah laka bi-iiqaaf sayyaaratika hunaa
You haven't put money in the parking meter	لم تضع نقودا في عداد الموقف lam tada' nuquudan fii 'addad al-mawqif
Your lights aren't working	مصابيحك لا تعمل masaabiihuka laa ta'mal
You'll have to pay a fine	عليك بدفع خطية بقيمة 'alayka bi-dafi' khatiyya bi-qiimat
Do you want to pay now?	هل تريد ان تدفع الآن؟ hal turiid an tadfa'a al-aan?
You'll have to pay now	يجب عليك ان تدفع الآن yajibu 'alyaka an tadfa'a al-aan

I don't speak Arabic	انا لا اتكلم العربية anaa laa atakallamu al-'arabiyya
I didn't see the sign	لم ار العلامة lam ara al-'alaama

I don't understand what ____ it says	لا افهمه ما تعنيه laa afahamu maa ta'niihi
I was only doing... ____ kilometers an hour	كنت اسوق بسرعة...كيلومتر في الساعة kuntu asuuqu bisur'at...kiilumatr fii as-saa'a
I'll have my car checked ____	أريد ان افحص سيارتي uriidu an afhasa sayyaaratii
I was blinded by oncoming ____ lights	أعمى عيني ضوء السيارات المقابلة a'maa 'aynii daw' as-sayyaaraat al-muqaabila

أين حصل هذا ؟ ayna hasala haadha?	Where did it happen?
ما المفقود ؟ maa l-mafquud?	What's missing?
ماذا اخذ منك؟ maadha ukhidha minka?	What's been taken?
هل يمكن ان ارى بطاقتك الشخصية / اية اثباتات شخصية؟ hal yumkin an araa bitaaqataka ash-shaksiyya / ayyat ithbaataat shakhsiyya?	Could I see your identity card / some identification?
متى حصل ذلك؟ mataa hasala dhaalik?	What time did it happen?
هل يوجد اي شهود ؟ hal yuujad ay shuhuud?	Are there any witnesses?
وقع هنا لو سمحت waqqi' hunaa law samahta	Sign here, please
هل تحتاج الى مترجم؟ hal tahtaaju ilaa mutarjim?	Do you want an interpreter?

14

At the police station

I want to report a collision / missing person / rape	اريد ان اخبر عن حادث تصادم/شخص مفقود /اغتصاب uriidu an ukhbira 'an haadith tasaadum / shakhs mafquud / ightisaab
Could you make a statement, please?	هل يمكن ان تكتب تصريحا من فضلك؟ hal yumkin an taktuba tasriihan min fadlik?

Could I have a copy for _____ the insurance?	هل يمكن ان احصل على نسخة لشركة التأمين؟
	hal yumkin an ahsula 'alaa nuskha li-sharikat at-ta'miin?
I've lost everything _____	فقدت كل شيء
	faqadtu kulla shay'
I've no money left, I'm _____ desperate	لم تبق لدي اية نقود انا في وضع حرج
	lam tabqa ladayya ayyat nuquud anaa fii wad'in harijin
Could you lend me a _____ little money?	هل يمكن ان تقرضني بعض المال؟
	hal yumkin an tuqridanii ba'da l-maal?
I'd like an interpreter _____	أحتاج إلى مترجم
	ahtaaju ilaa mutarjim
I'm innocent _____	أنا بريء
	anaa barii'
I don't know anything _____ about it	لا أعرف اي شيء عنه/عنها
	laa a'rifu ay shay' 'anhu / 'anhaa
I want to speak to someone _____ from the American embassy	اريد ان اتحدث الى شخص من السفارة الامريكية
	uriidu an atahaddatha ilaa shakhsin min as-safaara al-amariikiyya
I want a lawyer who _____ speaks...	اريد محاميا يتكلم اللغة...
	uriidu muhaamiyan yatakallamu al-lugha...

15

Word list

15

Word list: English – Arabic

• The following word list is meant to supplement the chapters in this book. Some of the words not on this list can be found elsewhere in this book. Food items can be found in Section 4.7, the parts of car from pages 64-65, the parts of a motorcycle / bicycle on page 70-71 and camping/backpacking equipment on page 88-89.

A

about	حوالي/تقريبا	hawaalay / taqriiban
above	أعلى/فوق	fawq / a'laa
abroad	في خارج البلاد	fii khaarij al-bilaad
accident	حادث	haadith
adaptor	وصلة	wasla
address	عنوان	'unwaan
admission	دخول	dukhuul
admission price	رسم الدخول	rasm ad-ukhuul
adult	كهل، بالغ	baaligh, kahl
advice	نصيحة	nasiiha
airplane	طائرة	taa'ira
after	بعد	ba'd
afternoon	مساء	massa'
aftershave	كولونيا	kulunya
again	مرة اخرى	marra ukhraa
against	ضد/مقابل	muqaabil / did
age	عمر	'umr
AIDS	أيدز	aydiz
air conditioning	تبريد	tabriid
airmail	بريد جوي	bariid jawwii
air mattress	سرير هوائي	sariir hawaa'ii
airplane	طائرة	taa'ira
airport	مطار	mataar
alarm	إنذار	indhaar
alarm clock	ساعة تنبيه	saa'at tanbiih
alcohol	خمر/كحول	kuhuul / khamr
all day	كل اليوم	kul al-yawm
all the time	طول الوقت	tuul al-waqt
allergy	حساسية	hassasiyya
alone	وحيدا	wahiidan
altogether	جميعا	jamii'an
always	دائما	daa'iman
ambulance	سيارة إسعاف	sayyaarat is'aaf
America	أمريكا	amariikaa

Word list

15

American	امريكي	amariikii
amount	كمية	kammiyya
amusement park	حديقة	hadiiqa
anesthetic (general)	تخدير كامل	takhdiir kaamili
anesthetic (local)	تخدير موضعي	takhdiir mawdi'ii
angry	منفعل	munfa'il
animal	حيوان	hayawaan
ankle	كعب	ka'ib
answer	جواب (رد)	jawaab (rad)
ant	نمله	namla
antibiotics	مضاد حيوي	mudaad hayawii
antifreeze	مضاد للتجميد	mudaad lit-tajmiid
antique	قديم	qadiim
antiques	قديم	qadiim
antiseptic	مضاد للعفونة	mudaad lil-'ufuuna
anus	الشرج (المخرج)	ash-sharj (al-makhraj)
apartment	شقه للسكن	shaqqa lis-sakan
aperitif	مشهي	mushahhii
apologies	اعتذار	i'tidhaar
apple	تفاحة	tuffaaha
apple juice	عصير تفاح	'asiir tuffaah
appointment	موعد	maw'id
April	نيسان	naysaan
architecture	هندسة معمارية	handasa mi'maariya
area	منطقة/مساحة	masaaha / mintaqa
area code	ترقيم بريدي	tarqiim bariidii
area code	مفتاح المنطقة	miftaah al-mintaqa
arm	ذراع	dhiraa'
arrange	يرتب	yurattib
arrive	يصل	yasil
arrow	سهم	sahm
art	فن	fan
art gallery	معرض للفنون	ma'rad lil-funun
artery	شريان	sharayaan
article	مقال	maqaal
artificial respiration	التنفس الاصطناعي	at-tanaffus al-istinaa'ii
ashtray	منفضة سجائر	minfadat sajaa'ir
ask	يسأل	yas'al
ask for	يطلب	yatlub
aspirin	اسبرين	asbariin
assault	اعتداء	i'tidaa'

assorted	مصنف	musannaf
at home	في البيت	fii al-bayt
at night	في الليل	fii al-layl
at the back	في الخلف	fii al-khalf
at the front	في الامام	fii al-amaam
at the latest	على الاقل	'alaa al-qal
aubergine	باذنجان	baadhinjaan
August	آب	aab
Australia	استراليا	ustiraaliyaa
Australian	استرالي	ustiraalii
automatic	اوتوماتيكي/ألي	aali / utumaatiikii
autumn	الخريف	al-khariif
awake	مستيقظ	mustayqiz
awning	الظل	az-zill

B

baby	رضيع/طفل	radii' / tifl
baby food	طعام طفل	ta'aam tifl
babysitter	حاضنة	haadina
back (part of body)	ظهر	zahr
back (rear)	خلف	khalf
backpack	حقيبة ظهر	haqibat zahr
backpacker	سائح مترجل	saa'ih mutarrajil
bad (rotting)	فاسد	faasid
bad (terrible)	سيء	sayyi'
bag	حقيبة	haqiiba
baker	خباز	khabbaaz
balcony	شرفة	shurfa
ball	كرة	kura
ballpoint pen	قلم جاف	qalam jaaf
banana	موز	mawz
bandage	ضماد	dimaad
bandaids	ضمادة	damaada
bangs	ضربة شديدة	darba shadiida
bank (finance)	مصرف	masraf
bank (river)	ضفة	diffa
bar (café)	بار	baar
barbecue	شواء في الهواء الطلق	shiwaa'fii al-hawaa' at-talq
basketball	كرة السلة	kurat as-salla
bath	حمام	hammaam
bathmat	فرشة باب الحمام	farshat baab al-hammaam
bathrobe	رداء حمام	ridaa' hammam

Word list

15

bathroom	غرفة حمام ghurfat al-hammaam
bath towel	منشفة حمام minshafat hammaam
battery	بطارية battaariyya
beach	ساحل saahil
beans	فاصوليا faasuuliya
beautiful	جميل jamiil
bed	فراش firaash
bedding	مفروشات السرير mafruushaat as-sariir
bee	نحلة nahla
beef	لحم بقر lahm baqar
beer	بيرة biira
begin	يبدأ yabda'
behind	خلف khalf
belt	حزام hizaam
berth	رصيف ميناء rasiif miinaa'
better (to get)	حسن hasan
bicycle	دراجة هوائية darraja hawaa'iyya
bikini	البيكيني al-bikiinii
bill	فاتورة fatuura
billiards	بليارد bilyaard
birthday	عيد الميلاد iid al-miilaad
biscuit	بسكويت baskawiit
bite	لدغه ladgha
bitter	مر mur
black	أسود aswad
black and white	أسود و أبيض aswad wa abyad
black eye	عين سوداء 'ayn sawdaa'
bland (taste)	بلا طعم bilaa ta'am
blanket	بطانية battaaniyya
bleach	مبيض mubayyid
bleed	ينزف yanzif
blind (can't see)	اعمى a'maa
blind (on window)	ستارة sitaara
blister	بثور جلدية buthuur jildiyya
blond	اشقر ashkar
blood	دم dam
blood pressure	ضغط الدم daght ad-dam
bloody nose	نزيف أنف naziif anf
blouse	بلوزة baluuza
blue	أزرق azraq
boat	قارب aqaarib
body	جسم jism

boiled	مغلي maghlii
bone	عظم 'azm
book	كتاب kitaab
booked, reserved	محجوز mahjuuz
booking office	مكتب الحجز maktab hajz
bookshop	مكتبة maktaba
border	حدود huduud
bored	سئم (ضجر) sa'im (dajir)
boring	ممل mumil
born	مولود mawluud
borrow	يستعير yasta'iir
botanic gardens	حدائق نباتية hadaa'iq nabaatiyya
both	كلاهما kilaahuma
bottle (baby's)	قنينة طفل qinniinat tifl
bottle (wine)	قنينة qinniina
bottle-warmer	مسخن قنينة musakhin qinniina
box	صندوق sunduuq
box office	صندوق بريد sunduuq bariid
boy	ولد walad
boyfriend	صديق sadiiq
bra	صدرية sadriyya
bracelet	سوار siwaar
braised	مطبوخ matbukh
brake	مكابح/فرامل faraamil / makaabih
brake oil	زيت فرامل zayt faraamil
bread	خبز khubz
break	استراحة istiraaha
breakfast	فطور fatuur
breast	ثدي thadii
breast milk	حليب ثدي haliib thadii
bridge	جسر jisr
briefs	ملخص mulakhas
bring	يجلب yajlib
brochure	منشور manshuur
broken	عاطل/مكسور maksuur / 'aatil
bronze	نحاس/برونز brunz / nuhaas
broth	حساء hisaa'
brother	أخ akh
brown	بني bunnii
bruise	رضض radad
brush	فرشاة furshaat
bucket	سطل satl

buffet	خزانة	khizaana
bugs	بق	baq
building	بناية	binaaya
bun	تسريحة	tasriiha
burglary	سطو (سرقة)	satw (sariqa)
burn (injury)	حرق	harq
burn (verb)	يحترق/يحرق	yuhriq / yahtariq
burnt	محروق	mahruuq
bus	حافلة (باص)	haafila (baas)
bus station	محطة حافلات (باصات)	mahattat haafilaat (baasaat)
bus stop	موقف حافلة (باص)	mawkif haafila (baas)
business card	كارت	kaart
business class	درجة أعمال	darajat a'maal
business trip	رحلة عمل	rihlat 'amal
busy (schedule)	مشغول	mashghuul
busy (traffic)	ازدحام	izdihaam
butane	غاز البوتان	gaaz al-buutan
butcher	قصاب (جزار)	qassaab (jazaar)
butter	زبدة	zubda
button	زر	zirr
by airmail	بالبريد الجوي	bil-bariid al-jawwii
by phone	بالتليفون	bit-tilifuun

c

cabbage	ملفوف	malfuuf
cabin	كوخ	kuukh
cake	كعك	ka'k
call (phonecall)	مكالمة	mukaalama
call (to phone)	يتصل	yattasil
called	اتصل	ittasala
camera	كاميرا	kaamira
camping	مخيم	mukhayyam
can opener	مفتاح علب	miftaah 'ulab
cancel	يلغي	yulghii
candle	شمعة	sham'a
candy	حلوى	halwaa
car	سيارة	sayyaara
cardigan	سترة صوف	sutrat suuf
car documents	اوراق السيارة	awraaq as-sayyaara
careful	حذر	hadhir
carpet	سجادة	sajjaada

carriage	عربة	'araba
carrot	جزر	jazar
car seat (child's)	مقعد طفل	maq'ad tifl
cartridge	خرطوشة	khartuusha
car trouble	عطب في السيارة	'atab fii as-sayyaara
cash	نقدي/فلوس	naqdii / fuluus
cash card	بطاقة نقد	bitaaqat naqd
cash desk	مكتب تصريف	maktab tasriif
cash machine	آلة تصريف	aalat tasriif
casino	كازينو	kaziinu
cassette	شريط	shariit
cat	قطة	qitta
catalog	كتالوغ	katalugh
cauliflower	قرنبيط	qarnabiit
cause	سبب	sabab
cave	كهف	kahf
CD	قرص	qurs
CD-ROM	مشغل أقراص	mushaghil aqraas
celebrate	يحتفل	yahtafil
cemetery	مقبرة	maqbara
center (middle)	مركز	markaz
center (of city)	مركز المدينة	markaz al-madiina
centimeter	سنتيميتر	sintimitar
central heating	تدفئة مركزية	tadfi'a markaziyya
central locking	قفل مركزي	qifl markazii
certificate	شهادة/وثيقة	wathiiqa / shahaada
chair	كرسي	kursii
chambermaid	خادمة فندق	khaadima funduq
champagne	شمبانيا	shimbaaniya
change, swap	يصرف	yusarrif
change (money)	صرف	sarf
change (trains)	تغيير	taghyiir
change the baby's diaper	يغير حفاظ الطفل	yughayyir haffaz ati-tifl
change the oil	يغير الزيت	yughayyir az-zayt
charter flight	رحلة جوية مؤجرة	rihla jawwiyyaa mu'ajjara
chat	دردشة	dardasha
checked luggage	فحص الحقائب	fahs al-haqaa'ib
check, bill	تدقيق	tadqiiq
check (verb)	فحص	fahs
check in	النزول بالفندق	an-nuzuul bil-funduq
check out	مغادرة الفندق	mughadarat al-funduq

cheers!	صحتين	sahtiin
cheese	جبن	jubn
chef	كبير الطباخين	kabiir at-tabbaakhiin
chess	شطرنج	shitranj
chewing gum	علك	'ilk
chicken	دجاجة	dajaaja
child	طفل	tifl
child's seat (in car)	مقعد الطفل	maq'ad tifl
chilled	مثلج/مجمد	mujammad / muthallaj
China	ذقن	dhaqn
chocolate	شوكلاتة	shuukalaata
choose	اختار	ikhtaar
chopsticks	أعواد صينية	a'waad siiniyya
church	كنيسة	kaniisa
church service	صلاة الكنيسة	salaat al-kaniisa
cigar	سيجار	siijaar
cigarette	سيجارة	siijaara
circle	دائرة	daa'ira
circus	سيرك	siirk
citizen	مواطن	muwaatin
city	مدينة	madiina
clean	نظيف	naziif
clean (verb)	ينظف	yunazzif
clearance (sale)	تصفية	tasfiya
clock	ساعة جدران	saa'at juduraan
closed	مغلق	mughlaq
closed off (road)	مغلق	mughlaq
clothes	ملابس	malaabis
clothes hanger	تعليقة ملابس	ta'liqah malaabis
clothes dryer	مجفف ملابس	mujaffif malaabis
clothing	ملابس/ثياب	malaabis / thiyaab
clutch (car)	دواسة القابض	dawaasat l-qaabid
coat (jacket)	سترة/جاكيت	jakiet / sitra
coat (overcoat)	معطف	mi'taf
cockroach	صرصور	sarsuur
cocoa	كاكاو	kakaw
coffee	قهوه	qahwa
cold (not hot)	بارد	baarid
cold, flu	الإنفلونزا	influwanza
collar	باقة	baaqa
collarbone	الترقوة	at-turquwa
colleague	زميل	zamiil

collision	تصادم	tasaadum
cologne	عطر	'itr
color	لون	lawn
colored	ملون	mulawwan
comb	مشط	musht
come	تعال	ta'aala
come back	ارجع	irja'
compartment	(جناح) مقصورة	maksuura (janaah)
complaint	شكوى	shakwaa
completely	تماما	tamaaman
compliment	إكمال	ikmaal
computer	حاسوب/كمبيوتر	kambyuutar / haasuub
concert	حفلة موسيقية	hafla muusiiqiyya
concert hall	قاعة غناء	qaa'at ghinaa'
concierge	حارس	haaris
concussion	رجة	rajja
condensed milk	حليب مكثف	haliib mukathaf
condom	غطاء مطاطي	ghitaa' mattaatii
confectionery	حلويات	halawiyyaat
congratulations!	مبروك/تهانينا	tahaaniinaa / mabruuk
connection (transport)	رحلة متممة	rihla mutammima
constipation	قبض	qabid
consulate	قنصلية	qunsiliyya
consultation (by doctor)	إستشارة	istishaara
contact lens	عدسات	'adasaat
contagious	معدي	mu'dii
contraceptive pill	حبوب منع الحمل	hubuub man' al-haml
cook (person)	طباخ	tabbakh
cook (verb)	يطبخ	yatbukh
cookie	بسكويت	baskawiit
copper	نحاسي	nuhaasii
copy	نسخة	nuskha
corkscrew	مفتاح/مبرام	miftaah / mibraam
corner	ركن	rukn
cornflower	دقيق الذرة	daqiiq adh-dhura
correct	صحيح	sahiih
correspond	يراسل	yuraasil
corridor	ممر	mamar
cosmetics	مواد تجميل	mawaad tajmiil
costume	زي	zay

Word list

15

cot	سرير طفل sariir tifl
cotton	قطن qutn
cotton wool	صوف قطني suuf qutnii
cough	كحة/سعال su'aal / kahha
cough (verb)	(يكح) يسعل yas'ul (yakuh)
cough syrup	شراب كحة sharaab kahha
counter	ضد/عكس 'aks / did
country (nation)	بلد balad
country (rural area)	ريف riif
country code	الترقيم البريدي للبلد at-tarqiim al-bariidii lil-balad
courgette	كوسة kuusa
course of treatment	فترة علاج fitrat 'ilaaj
cousin	ابن عم/بنت عم ibn 'am / bint 'am
crab	سرطان البحر sarataan al-bahr
cracker	كسارة kassaara
cream	قشطة qishta
credit card	بطاقة اعتماد bitaaqat i'timaad
crime	جريمة jariima
crockery	ادوات فخارية adawaat fakhariyya
cross (road, river)	تقاطع taqaatu'
crossroad	تقاطع طرق taqaatu' turuq
crutch	عكاز 'ukkaaz
cry	بكاء bukaa'
cubic meter	متر مكعب mitr muka'ab
cucumber	خيار khiyaar
cuddly toy	لعبة مسلية lu'ba musalliya
cuff	الكم al-kumm
cufflinks	زر كم القميص zirr kum al-qamiis
cup	كوب kuub
curly	مجعد muja'ad
current (electric)	تيار tayyaar
curtains	ستائر sataa'ir
cushion	وسادة wisaada
custom	عادة 'aada
customs	جمارك jamaarik
cut (injury)	جرح jurh
cut (verb)	يقطع yaqta'
cutlery	لوازم المائدة lawaazim al-maa'ida
cycling	سباق الدراجات sibaaq ad-darraajaat

D

| dairy products | لبنيات labaniyyaat |

damage	(خراب) ضرر	darar (kharaab)
dance	يرقص	yarqus
dandruff	قشرة	qishra
danger	خطر	khatar
dangerous	خطير	khatiir
dark	ظلام	zalaam
date	تاريخ	taariikh
date of birth	تاريخ الميلاد	taariikh miilaad
daughter	بنت	bint
day	يوم	yawm
day after tomorrow	بعد غد	ba'da ghad
day before yesterday	امس الأول	amsi al-awwal
dead	ميت	mayyit
deaf	اطرش	atrash
decaffeinated	خال من الكافايين	khaalin min l-kaafiin
December	كانون الاول	kaanuun ath-thaanii
declare (customs)	يصرح	yusarrih
deep	عميق	'amiiq
deep freeze	تجمد عميق	tajammud 'amiiq
deep-sea diving	الغوص في أعماق البحار	al-ghaws fii a'maaq al-bihaar
defecate	يتغوط	yataghawwat
degrees	درجات	darajaat
delay	تأخير	ta'khiir
delicious	لذيذ	ladhiidh
dentist	طبيب أسنان	tabiib asnaan
dentures	طقم اسنان	taqum asnaan
deodorant	معطر	mu'attir
department store	محل تجاري	mahall tijaarii
departure	مغادرة	mughaadara
departure time	وقت المغادرة	waqt al-mughaadara
depilatory cream	مستحضر مزيل الشعر	mustahdir muziil lish-sha'r
deposit (for safe-keeping)	وديعة/امانة	amaana / wadii'a
deposit (in bank)	يودع	yuudi'
desert	صحراء	sahraa'
dessert	حلويات	halawiyyaat
destination	مقصد/مصير	masiir / maqsad
detergent	مادة مطهرة	maadda mutahhira
develop (photo)	تحميض	tahmiid
diabetic	سكري	sukkarii

dial	طلب رقم على الهاتف talab raqm 'alaa al-haatif
diamond	ألماس almaas
diaper	حفاظ طفل haffaz tifl
diarrhea	اشهال ishhaal
dictionary	قاموس qaamuus
diesel oil	زيت الديزل zayt ad-diizil
diet	غذاء ghidhaa'
difficulty	صعوبة su'uuba
dining car	عربة طعام 'arabat ta'aam
dining room	غرفة الطعام ghurfat at-ta'aam
dinner	عشاء 'ashaa'
direction	اتجاه ittijaah
direct flight	طيران مباشر tayaraan mubaashir
directly	مباشر mubaasharatan
dirty	وسخ wasikh
disabled	معاق mu'aaq
disco	ديسكو diskuu
discount	تخفيض takhfiid
dish	طبق/صحن sahin / tabaq
dish of the day	طبق اليوم tabaq al-yawm
disinfectant	مبيد حشرات mubid hasharaat
distance	مسافة masaafa
distilled water	ماء مقطر maa' muqattar
disturb	يزعج yuz'ij
disturbance	ازعاج iz'aaj
dive	يغوص yaghuus
diving	الغوص al-ghaws
diving board	منصة الغوص manassat al-ghaws
diving gear	لاوازم الغوص lawaazim al-ghaws
divorced	مطلق mutallaq
dizzy	(دوخة) دوار duwaar (dawha)
do	يعمل ya'mal
doctor	طبيب tabiib
dog	كلب kalb
do-it-yourself store	محل خدمات ذاتية mahal khadamaat dhaatiyya
doll	دمية dumiya
domestic	محلي mahallii
done (cooked)	مطبوخ matbuukh
do not disturb	الرجاء عدم الإزعاج ar-rajaa' 'adam al-izaaj
door	باب baab

double	ضعف	di'f
down	اسفل	asfal
drapes	ستائر	sataa'ir
draught	جفاف	jafaaf
dream (verb)	يحلم	yahlum
dress	يلبس/بدلة	badla / yalbas
dressing gown	عباءة	'abaa'a
dressing table	منضدة	mindada
drink (alcoholic)	خمر (مشروب)	khamr (mashruub)
drink (refreshment)	شراب	sharaab
drink (verb)	يشرب	yashrab
drinking water	ماء شرب	maa' shurb
drive	يسوق	yasuuq
driver	سائق	saa'iq
driver's license	رخصة سياقة	rukhsat siyaaqa
drugstore	مخزن ادوية	makhzan adwiya
drunk	سكران	sakraan
dry	جاف	jaaf
dry (verb)	يجفف/يجف	yujaffif / yajuf
dry-clean	غسل وتجفيف	ghasl wa tajfiif
drycleaners	غسل جاف	ghasl jaff
duck	بطة	batta
during	خلال	khilaal
during the day	خلال اليوم	khilaal al-yawm
duty (tax)	رسم جمركي	rasm jumrukii
duty-free goods	بضائع غير خاضعة للرسم الجمركي	badaa'i' ghayr khaadi'a lir-rasm al-jumrukii
duty-free shop	دكان غير خاضع للرسم الجمركي	dukaan khaadi' lir-rasm al-jumrukii
DVD	دي في دي	dii vii dii

E

ear	أذن	udhun
earache	ألم في الاذن	alam fii al-udhun
ear drops	قترة للاذن	qatra lil-udhun
early	مبكر	mubakkir
earrings	الدخل	dakhl
earth	أرض	ard
earthenware	خزف	khazaf
east	شرق	sharq
easy	سهل	sahl
eat	يأكل	ya'kul

economy class	درجة اقتصادية	daraja iqtiṣaadiyya
eczema	اكزما	akzima
eel	سمكة الأنقليس	samakat al-anqaliis
egg	بيض	bayd
eggplant	باذنجان	baadhinjaan
electric	كهربائي	kahrabaa'ii
electricity	كهرباء	kahrabaa'
electronic	الكتروني	ilikituunii
elephant	فيل	fiil
elevator	مصعد كهربائي	miṣ'ad kahrabaa'ii
email	بريد الكتروني	bariid ilikituunii
embassy	سفارة	saraara
embroidery	تطريز	taṭriiz
emergency brake	مكابح طوارئ	makaabiḥ ṭawaari'
emergency exit	مخرج طوارئ	makhraj ṭawaari'
emergency phone	هاتف طوارئ	haatif ṭawaari'
emperor	امبراطور	imbiraaṭuur
empress	امبراطورة	imbiraaṭuura
empty	فارغ	faarigh
engaged (on the phone)	مشغول	mashguul
engaged (to be married)	مخطوبة/مخطوب	makhtuub / makhtuuba
England	انجلترا	ingiltaraa
English	انجليزي	ingliizii
enjoy	يتمتع	yatamatta'
enquire	استفسار/يستفسر	istifsaar / yastafsir
envelope	ظرف	ẓarf
escalator	درج ميكانيكي	daraj miikaaniikii
escort	يرافق	yuraafiq
essential	اساسي	asaasii
evening	مساء	masaa'
evening wear	لباس المساء	libaas al-masaa'
event	مناسبة/حدث	ḥadath / munaasaba
everything	كل شيء	kull shay'
everywhere	في كل مكان	fii kull makaan
examine	يفحص	yafḥaṣ
excavation	تنقيب	tanqiib
excellent	ممتاز	mumtaasz
exchange	يصرف/يبدل عملة	yubaddil 'amila / yuṣarrif
exchange office	مكتب تصريف	maktab taṣriif
excursion	رحلة	riḥla

exhibition	معرض	ma'rad
exit	مخرج	maqraj
expenses	مصاريف/نفقات	masaariif / nafaqaat
expensive	غال	ghaalin
explain	يشرح	yashrah
express	يعبر	ya'bur
external	خارجي	khaarijii
eye	عين	ayn
eye drops	قطرة للعين	qatra lil-ayn
eye specialist	أخصائي عيون	akhissaa'ii uyuun

F

fabric	قماش	qumaash
face	وجه	wajh
factory	مصنع	masna'
fall (season)	خريف	khariif
fall (verb)	يسقط	yasqut
family	عائلة	'aa'ila
famous	مشهور	mashhuur
fan	مروحة	marwaha
far away	بعيد	baiid
farm	مزرعة	mazra'a
farmer	فلاح	fallah
fashion	زي	zay
fast	سريع	sarii'
father	اب	ab
father-in-law	الحمو	al-hamuw
fault	خطأ	khata'
fax	فاكس	faaks
February	شباط	shubaat
feel	يشعر	yash'ur
feel like	يود	yawadd
fence	سور	suur
ferry	عبارة/سفينة	safiina / 'abbaara
fever	حرارة/حمى	hummaa / haraara
fiancé	خطيب	khatiib
fiancée	خطيبة	khatiiba
fill	يملأ	yamla'
filling (dental)	حشوة	hashwa
filling (in food)	مملوء	mamluu'
fill out (form)	يملأ	yamla'
film (cinema)	فلم	film

film (photo)	فلم	film
filter	مصفاة (فلتر)	misfaat (filtar)
filter cigarette	سيجار فلتر	sijaar filtar
fine (good)	جيد (حسن)	jayyid (hasan)
fine (money)	خطية/غرامة	gharaama / khatiyya
finger	إصبع	isbi'
fire	حريق/نار	naar / hriiq
fire alarm	منبه حريق	munabbih hariiq
fire department	الاطفاء	al-itfaa'
fire escape	مهرب حريق	mahrab hariiq
fire extinguisher	آلة اطفاء النار	aalat itfaa' al-naar
first	اول	awwal
first aid	اسعافات اولية	is'aafaat awwaliyya
first class	درجة أولى	daraja uulaa
fish	سمك	samak
fish (verb)	يصطاد السمك	yastaad as-samak
fishing rod	عصا الصيد	'asaa as-sayd
fitness club	نادي لياقة	naadii liyaaqa
fitness training	تدريب لياقة	tadriib liyaaqa
fitting room	غرفة المقاييس	ghurfat al-maqaayiis
fix (puncture)	يصلح	yuslih
flag	علم	'alam
flash (camera)	ضوء (فلاش)	daw' (flash)
flashlight	ضوء متقطع	daw' mutaqatti'
flatulence	تطبيل	tatbiil
flavor	نكهة	nukha
flavoring	مادة منكهة	maadda munakkiha
flea	برغوث	barghuuth
flea market	سوق البرغوث	suuq al-barghuuth
flight	رحلة طيران	rihlat tayaraan
flight number	رقم الرحلة	raqam ar-rihla
flood	فيضان	fayadaan
floor	أرضية/طابق	ardiyya/taabaq
flour	طحين	tahiin
flu	الإنفلونزا	al-influwanza
flush (verb)	تغسل	yaghsil
fly (insect)	ذبابة	dhubaaba
fly (verb)	يطير	yatiir
fog	ضباب	dabaab
foggy	ضبابي	dabaabii
folklore	فلكلور	fuliklor
follow	يتبع	yatba'

food (groceries)	مواد غذائية mawaad ghidhaa'iyya
food (meal)	(غذاء) طعام ta'aam (ghidhaa')
food court	ساحة مطاعم saahat mataa'im
food poisoning	تسمم غذائي tasammum ghidhaa'ii
foot	قدم qadam
foot brake	كسر القدم kasr al-qadam
forbidden	يمنع/يحرم yuharrim / yamna'
forehead	جبين jabiin
foreign	أجنبي/غريب ghariib / ajnabii
forget	ينسى yansaa
fork	شوكة shawka
form	استمارة istimaara
formal dress	زي رسمي zay rasmii
forward (letter)	يرسل yusrsil
fountain	نافورة nafuura
frame	أطار itaar
free (no charge)	مجاني majjaanii
free (unoccupied)	حر hur
free time	وقت فراغ waqt faraagh
freeze	(تجمد) انجماد injimaad
french fries	مقليات فرنسية maqliyyat faransiyya
fresh	طازج taazij
Friday	الجمعة al-jumu'a
fried	مقلي maqlii
friend	صديق sadiiq
friendly	ودي widdii
frightened	مذعور madh'uur
fringe (hair)	القصة al-qussa
frozen	مجمد mujammad
fruit	فواكه fawaakih
fruit juice	عصير فواكه 'asiir fawaaqih
frying pan	مقلاة maqlaat
full	مملوء/شبعان shab'aan / mamluu'
fun	مرح/لهو marah / lahw
funeral	جنائز janaa'iz

G

gallery	بهو (صالة) bahw (saala)
game	لعبة lu'ba
garage (car repair)	ورشة تصليح warshat tasliih
garbage	زبالة zibaala
garlic	ثوم thuum

Word list

15

garden	حديقة ḥadiiqa
garment	ثوب thawb
gas (for heating)	غاز ghaaz
gasoline	بنزين banziin
gas station	محطة وقود maḥattat waquud
gate	بوابة bawwaaba
gear (car)	التروس at-turuus
gem	جوهرة jawhara
gender	الجنس al-jins
get off	يخرج/ينزل yakhruj / yanzil
get on	يصعد yaṣ'ad
gift	هدية hadiyya
ginger	زنجبيل zanjabiil
girl	بنت bint
girlfriend	صديقة ṣadiiqa
given name	الاسم al-ism
glass (for drinking)	كأس/كوب kuub / ka's
glass (material)	زجاج zujaaj
glasses	نظارات naẓẓaaraat
gliding	طيران شراعي ṭayaraan shiraa'ii
glossy (photo)	لامع laami'
gloves	قفازات quffaazaat
glue	صمغ ṣamagh
gnat	بعوضة ba'uuḍa
go	اذهب idhhab
go back	ارجع irji'
go out	اخرج ukhruj
gold	ذهب dhahab
golf	صولجان/غولف gulf / ṣawlajaan
golf course	ملعب الغولف mal'ab al-gulf
good afternoon	مساء الخير massa' al-khayr
goodbye	مع السلامة ma'a as-salaama
good evening	مساء الخير massa' al-khayr
good morning	صباح الخير ṣabaah al-khayr
good night	تصبح على خير tuṣbih 'alaa khayr
goose	اوزة iwazza
gram	غرام ghraam
grandchild	حفيد hafiid
granddaughter	حفيدة hafiida
grandfather	جد jad
grandmother	جدة jadda
grandparent	الجدان al-jaddaan

grandson	حفيد	hafiid
grape juice	عصير عنب	'asiir 'inab
grapes	عنب	'inab
grave	مقبرة	maqbara
gray	رمادي	ramaadii
graze (injury)	يرعى	yar'aa
greasy	مشحم	mushahham
green	أخضر	akhdar
greengrocer	خضار	khaddaar
greeting	تحية	tahiyya
grey-haired	ذو شعر رمادي	dhuu sha'r ramaadii
grilled	مشوي	mashwii
grocer	بقال	baqqaal
groceries	بقالة	biqaala
group	مجموعة	majmuu'a
guest house	بيت ضيافة	bayt diyaafa
guide (book)	دليل	daliil
guide (person)	مرشد/موجه	muwajjih / murshid
guided tour	رحلة مع مرشد	rihla ma'a murshid
guilt	إثم/ذنب	dhanb / ithm
gym	جمناستك	jumnaastik
gynecologist	أخصائي أمراض النساء	akhissaii amraad an-nisaa'

H

hair	شعر	sha'r
hairbrush	مشط	mushit
haircut	قصة شعر	qassat sha'r
hairdresser	حلاق	hallaaq
hairdryer	مجفف شعر	mujaffif sha'r
hairspray	رشاش شعر	rashaash sha'r
hairstyle	تسريحة شعر	tasriihat sha'r
half	نصف	nisf
half full	نصف مملوء	nisf mamluu'
hammer	مطرقة	mitraqa
hand	يد	yad
handbag	حقيبة يد	haqiibat yad
hand brake	فرامل يدوية	fraamil yadawiyya
handkerchief	منديل	mindiil
hand luggage	حقيبة يد	haqiiba yad
handmade	صنع يدوي	sun' yadawii
hand towel	منشفة	minshafa
happy	سعيد	sa'iid

Word list

15

harbor	ميناء	minaa'
hard (difficult)	صعب	sa'b
hard (firm)	قاسي/صلب	salb / qaasii
hardware store	متجر مواد معدنية	matjar mawaad ma'daniyya
hat	قبعة	qubba'a
hay fever	حمى القش	humma al-qash
head	رأس	ra's
headache	صداع	sudaa'
headlights	إضاءة امامية	idaa'a amaamiyya
health food shop	دكان اطعمة صحية	dukkaan at'ima sihhiyya
healthy	صحي	sihhii
hear	يسمع	yasma'
hearing aid	سماعات اذن	sammaa'aat udhun
heart	قلب	qalb
heart attack	أزمة قلبية	azma qalbiyya
heat	حرارة	haraara
heater	مدفأة	midfa'a
heavy	ثقيل	thaqiil
heel (of foot)	كعب	ka'b
heel (of shoe)	كعب	ka'b
hello	اهلا	ahlan
help	النجدة/مساعدة	musaa'ada / an-najda
helping (of food)	معونة	ma'uuna
hem	حافة	haafat
herbal tea	شاي الاعشاب	shaay al-'ashaab
herbs	اعشاب	'ashaab
here	هنا	hunaa
high	عال	'aalin
high chair	كرسي عال للأطفال	kursii 'aalii lil-atfaal
high tide	أعلى مستوى للمد	a'laa mustawaa lil-mad
highway	طريق سريع	tariiq sarii'
hiking	نزهة سير على الاقدام	nuzhat sayr 'alaa al-aqdaam
hiking boots	حذاء نزهة السير على الاقدام	hidhaa' nuzhat as-sayr 'alaa al-aqdaam
hip	ورك	warak
hire	يستأجر	yasta'jir
hitchhike	سفر تطفلي	safar tataffulii
hobby	هواية	hiwaaya
holdup	توقف	tawaqquf
holiday (festival)	عطلة	'utla
holiday (public)	عطلة	'utla
holiday (vacation)	إجازة	ijaaza

homesick	الحنين إلى الوطن al-haniin ila l-watan
honest	أمين amiin
honey	عسل 'asal
horizontal	أفقي ufuqii
horrible	كريه kariih
horse	حصان hisaan
hospital	مستشفى mustashfaa
hospitality	ضيافة diyaafa
hot (bitter, sharp)	حاد haad
hot (warm)	حار haar
hot spring	ربيع حار rabii' haar
hot-water bottle	قنينة ماء حار qinniinat maa' haar
hotel	فندق funduq
hour	ساعة saa'a
house	بيت bayt
houses of parliament	مقر البرلمان maqar al-barlamaan
how?	كيف؟ kayf?
how far?	كم المسافة؟ kam al-masaafa?
how long?	كم المدة؟ kam al-mudda?
how many?	كم؟ kam?
how much?	كم؟ kam?
hundred grams	مئة غرام mi'at ghraam
hungry	جائع (جوعان) jaa'i' (jaw'aan)
hurry	بسرعة/أسرع asri' / bisur'a
husband	زوج zawj
hut	كوخ kuukh

I

ice cream	بوظة buuza
ice cubes	مكعبات ثلج muka'abaat thalj
iced	مثلج muthallaj
ice-skating	تزلج على الجليد tazalluj 'alaa ath-thalj
idea	فكرة fikra
identification (card)	بطاقة شخصية bitaaqa shakhsiyya
identify	يتعرف yuta'arraf
ignition key	مفتاح قدح miftaah qadh
ill	مريض mariid
illness	مرض marad
imagine	يتخيل yatakhayyal
immediately	حالا haalan
important	مهم muhim

import duty	ضريبة الاستيراد	<u>d</u>ariibat al-istiiraad
impossible	مستحيل	musta<u>h</u>iil
improve	يحسن/يطور	yu<u>t</u>awwir / yu<u>h</u>assin
in	في	fii
indigestion	سوء هضم	suu' <u>h</u>adm
in-laws	الأنساب	al-ansaab
internet café	مقهى انترنيت	maqhaa interniit
in the evening	في المساء	fii al-masaa'
in the morning	في الصباح	fii a<u>s</u>-<u>s</u>abaa<u>h</u>
included	مشمول	ma<u>sh</u>muul
include in	يشمل	ya<u>sh</u>mal
indicate	يوضح	yuwa<u>dd</u>i<u>h</u>
indicator (car)	إشارة	i<u>sh</u>aara
inexpensive	رخيص	ra<u>kh</u>ii<u>s</u>
infection	إلتهاب	ilti<u>h</u>aab
infectious	معدي	mu'dii
inflammation	التهاب	ilti<u>h</u>aab
information	معلومات	ma'luumaat
information office	مكتب معلومات	maktab ma'luumaat
injection	حقنة	<u>h</u>uqna
injured	مجروح	majruu<u>h</u>
inner tube	أنبوب داخلي	unbuub da<u>kh</u>ilii
innocent	بريء	barii'
insect	حشرة	<u>h</u>a<u>sh</u>ara
insect bite	لدغة حشرة	lad<u>gh</u>at <u>h</u>a<u>sh</u>ara
insect repellant	مبيد حشرة	mubiid <u>h</u>a<u>sh</u>ara
inside	داخل	daa<u>kh</u>il
instructions	تعليمات	ta'liimaat
insurance	تأمين/ضمان	<u>d</u>amaan / ta'miin
intermission	فترة استراحة	fitrat istiraa<u>h</u>a
internal	داخلي	daa<u>kh</u>ilii
international	دولي	duwalii
interpreter	مترجم	mutarjim
intersection	تقاطع	taqaa<u>t</u>u'
introduce oneself	يقدم (يعرف)	yuqaddim (yu'arrif)
invite	يدعو	yad'uu
invoice	فاتورة	faatuura
iodine	اليود	al-yuud
Ireland	ايرلندا	iirlanda
iron (metal)	حديد	<u>h</u>adiid
iron (for clothes)	مكواة	mikwaat
iron (verb)	يكوي	yakwii

ironing board	لوح الكوي lawh kawii
island	جزيرة jaziira
itch	حكة hakka

J

jack (for car)	رافعة raafi'a
jacket	جاكيت (سترة) jaakiit (sutra)
jam	مربى murabba
January	كانون الثاني kanuun ath-thaanii
jaw	فك fak
jeans	جينز jeanz
jellyfish	قنديل البحر qindiil al-bahr
jeweler	صائغ saa'igh
jewelry	مجوهرات mujawharaat
job	شغل/وظيفة shughl / waziifa
jog	يركض yarkud
joke	نكتة nukta
journey	رحلة rihla
juice	عصير 'asiir
July	تموز tammuuz
June	حزيران huzayraan

K

kerosene	كيروسين kiirusiin
key	مفتاح miftaah
kidney	الكلى al-kilaa
kilogram	كيلوغرام kiloghraam
king	ملك malik
kiss	قبلة qubla
kiss (verb)	يقبل yuqabbil
kitchen	مطبخ matbakh
knee	ركبة rukba
knife	سكين sikiin
knit	يحوك yahuuk
know	يعرف ya'rif

L

lace (fabric)	زخرفة zakhrafa
laces (for shoes)	رباط حذاء ribaata al-hidhaa'
ladder	درج daraj
lake	بحيرة buhayra
lamb	خروف (حمل) kharuuf (haml)

Word list

15

lamp	مصباح	misbaah
land (ground)	أرض	ard
land (verb)	تخط (تنزل)	tahut (tanzil)
lane (of traffic)	مسار	masaar
language	لغة	lugha
large	كبير (واسع)	kabiir (waasi')
last (endure)	يستمر	yastamir
last (final)	آخر	aakhir
last night	الليلة الماضية	al-layla al-maadiya
late	متأخر	muta'akhir
later	فيما بعد	fiimaa ba'd
laugh	يضحك	yadhak
launderette	مؤسسة غسل وكوي	mu'assat ghasl wa kawii
laundry soap	صابون ملابس	saabun malaabis
law	قانون	qaanuun
lawyer	محامي	muhaamii
laxative	مسهل (ملين)	musahil (mulayyin)
leak	تسرب	tasarrub
leather	جلد	jild
leather goods	بضائع جلدية	badaa'i' jildiyya
leave	يغادر	yughaadir
left	يسار/متبقي	mutabaqqii / yasaar
left behind	نسي	nasiya
leg	ساق	saaq
leggings	غطاء الساقين	ghitaa' as-saaqayn
leisure	وقت فراغ	waqt
lemon	ليمون	laymuun
lend	يقرض	yuqrid
lens (camera)	عدسات	'adasaat
less	أقل	aqal
lesson	درس	dars
letter	حرف/رسالة	risaala / harf
lettuce	خس	khass
level crossing	معبر	ma'bar
library	مكتبة	maktaba
license	إجارة/رخصة	rukhsa / ijaaza
lie (be lying)	يكذب	yakdhib
lie (falsehood)	كذب	kadhib
lie down	يستلقي	yastalqii
lift (elevator)	مصعد	mis'ad
lift (in car)	توصيلة	tawsiila
light (lamp)	مصباح	misbah

light (not dark)	مضيء mudii'
light (not heavy)	خفيف khafiif
light bulb	مصباح misabah
lighter	قداحة qiddaha
lightning	البرق al-barq
like (verb)	يرغب (يحب) yuhib (yarghab)
line	خط khat
linen	كتان kittaan
lining	بطانة bitaana
liquor store	مخزن مشروبات makhzan mashruubaat
liqueur	مشروبات كحولية mashruubaat kuhuuliyya
listen	يصغي (يستمع) yusghii (yastami')
liter	لتر latr
literature	أدب adab
little (amount)	قليل qaliil
little (small)	صغير saghiir
live (alive)	يعيش ya'iish
live (verb)	يسكن yaskun
liver	الكبد al-kabid
lobster	جراد البحر jaraad al-bahr
local	محلي mahallii
lock	قفل/يقفل qufl / yaqfil
long	طويل tawiil
long-distance call	مكالمة بعيدة maukama ba'iida
look at	ينظر الى yanzur ilaa
look for	يبحث عن yabhath 'an
look-up	يبحث عن yabhath 'an
lose	يفقد yafqid
loss	خسارة (فقدان) khasaara (fiqdaan)
lost (can't find way)	مفقود mafquud
lost (missing)	ضائع daa'i'
lost and found office	مكتب الموجودات والمفقودات maktab al-mawjuudaat wa al-mafquudaat
lotion	مستحضر غسيل mustahdar ghasiil
loud	عال 'aalin
love	حب hub
love (verb)	يحب yuhib
low	منخفض munkhafid
low tide	أدنى مستوى للجزر adnaa mustawaa lil-jazr
LPG	غاز ghaz
luck	حظ haz
luggage	حقائب/أمتعة amti'a / haqaa'ib

Word list

15

171

luggage locker	خزانة الحقائب <u>kh</u>izaanat al-<u>h</u>aqaa'ib
lumps (sugar)	قطع السكر qi<u>t</u>a' as-sukkar
lunch	غداء <u>gh</u>idhaa'
lungs	الرئتان ar-ri'ataan

M

madam	(سيدة) مدام madam (sayyida)
magazine	مجلة majalla
mail (letters)	بريد bariid
mail (verb)	يرسل بالبريد yursil bil-bariid
main post office	مكتب البريد الرئيسي maktab al-briid ar-ra'iisii
main road	طريق رئيسي <u>t</u>ariiq ra'iisii
make, create	يخلق/يصنع ya<u>s</u>na' / ya<u>kh</u>laq
make an appointment	يحدد موعدا yu<u>h</u>addid maw'idan
make love	يمارس الجنس yumaaris al-jins
makeshift	بديل مؤقت badiil mu'aqqat
makeup	مكياج mikyaaj
man	رجل rajul
manager	مدير mudiir
mango	مانجا manja
manicure	صبغ اظافر <u>s</u>ub<u>gh</u> a<u>z</u>aafir
many	كثير ka<u>th</u>iir
map	خارطة <u>kh</u>aari<u>t</u>a
marble	مرمر marmar
March	آذار aa<u>dh</u>aar
margarine	زبدة zubda
marina	مرسى marsaa
marital status	الحالة المدنية al-<u>h</u>aala al-madaniyya
market	سوق suuq
married	متزوج mutazawwij
mass	كتلة kutla
massage	رسالة risaala
mat (on floor)	سجادة صغيرة sajaada <u>s</u>a<u>gh</u>iira
mat (on table)	قطعة قماش الطاولة qi<u>t</u>'at qumaa<u>sh</u> at-taawila
match	يوافق (يناسب) yuwaafiq (yunaasib)
matches	كبريت kabriit
May	أيار ayaar
maybe	ربما rubbamaa
mayonnaise	مايونيز maayuuniiz
mayor	محافظ mu<u>h</u>aafi<u>z</u>
meal	وجبة غذائية wajba <u>gh</u>idhaa'iyya

mean	يعني	ya'nii
measure	يقيس	yaqiis
measuring jug	مكيال	mikyaal
measure out	يقيس	yaqiis
meat	لحم	lahm
medication	علاج	'ilaaj
medicine	دواء	dawaa'
meet	يلتقي بـ	yaltaqii bi
melon	بطيخ (شمام)	battikh (shimmaam)
member	عضو	'udw
member of parliament	عضو برلمان	'udw barlamaan
membership card	بطاقة عضوية	bitaaqat 'udwiyya
mend	تصليح / يصلح	yuslih / tasliih
menstruate	تحيض	tahiid
menstruation	حيض	hayd
menu	قائمة المأكولات	qaa'imat al-ma'kuulaat
message	رسالة	risaala
metal	معدن	ma'dan
meter	متر	matr
meter (in taxi)	عداد	'addad
migraine	صداع الشقيقة	sudaa' ash-shaqiiqa
mild (taste)	لطيف	latiif
milk	حليب	haliib
millimeter	مليمتر	millimitr
mineral water	مياه معدنية	miyaah ma'daniyya
minute	دقيقة	daqiiqa
mirror	مرآة	mir'aat
miss (flight, train)	يتأخر عن	yata'akhar 'an
miss (loved one)	يشتاق	yashtaaq
missing	مفقود	mafquud
missing person	شخص مفقود	shakhis mafquud
mist	ضباب	dabaab
misty	غامض	ghamid
mistake	خطأ (غلطة)	khata' (ghalta)
mistaken	مخطيء	mukhti'
misunderstanding	سوء فهم	suu' fahm
mixed	ممزوج	mamzuuj
modern art	الفن الحديث	al-fan al-hadiith
moment	لحظة	lahza
monastery	دير	dayr
Monday	الاثنين	al-ithnayn

money	(فلوس) نقود	nuquud (fuluus)
monkey	قرد	qird
month	شهر	<u>sh</u>ahr
moon	قمر	qamr
moped	دراجة آلية	darraaja aaliya
mosquito	بعوضة	ba'u<u>d</u>a
mosquito net	شبكة بعوض	<u>sh</u>abakat ba'uu<u>d</u>
motel	فندق صغير	fundiq <u>s</u>a<u>gh</u>iir
mother	ام	um
mother-in-law	الحماة	al-<u>h</u>amaa
motorbike	دراجة نارية	darraaja naariya
motorboat	زورق مزود بمحرك	zawraq muzawwad bi-mu<u>h</u>arrak
mountain	جبل	jabal
mountain hut	كوخ جبلي	kuu<u>kh</u> jabalii
mouse	فأر	fa'r
mouth	فم	fam
MSG	رسالة	risaala
much	كثير	ka<u>th</u>iir
mud	طين	<u>t</u>iin
muscle	عضلة	'<u>ad</u>ala
muscle spasms	تقلص عضلي	taqallu<u>s</u> '<u>ad</u>alii
museum	متحف	mat<u>h</u>af
mushrooms	الفطر	al-fu<u>t</u>r
music	موسيقى	muusiiqaa

N

nail (finger)	ظفر	<u>z</u>ifr
nail (metal)	مسمار	mismaar
nail file	مبرد اظافر	mibrad a<u>z</u>aafir
nail scissors	مقص اظافر	miqa<u>s</u> a<u>z</u>aafir
naked	عار	'aarin
nappy, diaper	حفاظ طفل	<u>h</u>affa<u>z</u> <u>t</u>ifl
nationality	جنسية	jinsiyya
natural	طبيعي	<u>t</u>abii'ii
nature	طبيعة	<u>t</u>abii'a
nauseous	مقرف	muqurif
near	قرب	qurb
nearby	قريب	qariib
necessary	ضروري	<u>d</u>aruurii
neck	رقبة	raqaba
necklace	قلادة	qilaada
necktie	ربطة عنق	rab<u>t</u>at 'unuq

needle	إبرة ibra
negative (photo)	نيجاتيف الصور nijaatiif as-suwar
neighbor	جار jaar
nephew	ابن الاخت/ابن الاخ ibn al-akh / ibn al-ukht
never	أبد abadan
new	جديد jadiid
news	أخبار akhbaar
newspaper	صحيفة/جريدة sahiifa / jariida
news stand	كشك الصحف kushik as-suhuf
next	اللاحق/القادم al-laahiq / al-qaadim
next to	بالقرب من bilqurb
nice (person)	(جميل) طيب tayyib (jamiil)
nice (pleasant)	(ممتع) جميل jamiil (mumti')
niece	بنت الاخت/بنت الاخ bint al-akh / bint al-ukht
night	ليل layl
night duty	دوام ليلي dawaam laylii
nightclothes	ملابس ليلية malaabis layliyya
nightclub	نادي ليلي naadii laylii
nightdress	لباس ليلي libas laylii
nipple (bottle)	حلمة hilma
no	لا/كلا laa / kallaa
no entry	ممنوع الدخول mamnuu' ad-dukhuul
no thank you	لا شكرا لك laa shukran laka
noise	ضوضاء dawdaa'
nonstop (flight)	دون توقف duun tawaqquf
noodles	معكرونة ma'karuuna
no-one	لا احد laa ahad
normal	طبيعي tabii'ii
north	شمال shamaal
nose	انف anf
nosebleed	نزيف الانف naziif anf
nose drops	قطرة انف qatrat anf
notebook	دفتر ملاحظات daftar mulaahazaat
notepad	ورق ملاحظات waraq mulaahazaat
notepaper	دفتر ملاحظات daftar mulaahazaat
nothing	لا شيء laa shay'
November	تشرين الثاني tishriin ath-thaanii
nowhere	ليس في أي مكان laysa fii ay-makaan
number	رقم raqim
number plate	رقم السيارة raqim as-sayyaara
nurse	ممرضة mumarrida
nuts	فستق fustuq

Word list

o

occupation	وظيفة (شغل) waẓiifa (shughl)
October	تشرين الأول tishriin al-awwal
off (gone bad)	فاسد faasid
off (turned off)	يغلق (يطفيء) yughliq (yuṭfi')
offer	عرض arḍ
office	دائرة daa'ira
oil	زيت zayt
oil level	مستوى الزيت mustawaa az-zayt
ointment	مرهم marham
okay	نعم/لا بأس laa ba's / naam
old	قديم qadiim
on, at	عند/على 'alaa / inda
on (turned on)	مشغل/مفتوح maftuuḥ / musahghal
on board	راكب raakib
oncoming car	سيارة قادمة sayyaara qaadima
one-way ticket	تذكرة سفر رحلة واحدة tadhkirat safar riḥla waaḥida
one-way traffic	حركة مرور باتجاه واحد ḥarakat muruur bit-tijaah waaḥid
onion	بصل baṣal
on the left	على اليسار 'alaa al-yasaar
on the right	على اليمين 'alaa al-yamiin
on the way	في الطريق fii aṭ-ṭariiq
open	مفتوح maftuuḥ
open (verb)	يفتح yaftaḥ
operate (surgeon)	عملية جراحية 'amaliyya jiraaḥiyya
operator (telephone)	العامل بمركز الإتصالات al-'aamil bi-markaz al-ittisaalaat
opposite	مقابل/عكس 'aks / muqaabul
optician	نظاراتي naḍhaaraatii
orange (color)	برتقالي burtughalii
orange (fruit)	برتقال butughaal
order	رتبة/(طلب) أمر amr (talab) / rutba
order (verb)	يأمر ya'mur
other	آخر aakhar
other side	من جهة أخرى min jiha ukhraa
outside	خارج khaarij
overpass	معبر ma'bar
overseas	في الخارج fii al-khaarij
overtake	يتجاوز yatajaawaz
over there	هناك hunaak

oyster	محار mahhaar

P

packed lunch	وجبة معلبة wajba mu'allaba
page	صفحة safha
pain	ألم alam
painkiller	مسكن ألم musakkin alam
paint	صبغ/دهان sabgh / dihaan
painting	يصبغ yasbagh
pajamas	بيجامة biijaama
palace	مكان makaan
pan	مقلاة miqlaat
pane	لوح lawh
panties	سراويل saraawiil
pants	بنطلون bantaluun
pantyhose	جورب نسائي jawrab nisaa'ii
papaya	بابايا babaaya
paper	ورق waraq
paraffin oil	زيت البرافين zayt al-baraafiin
parasol	مظلة mizalla
parcel	طرد/رزمة ruzma / tard
pardon	عفوا 'afwan
parents	والدان waalidaan
park (gardens)	(حديقة) متنزه mutanazzah (hadiiqa)
park (verb)	يوقف السيارة yuqif as-sayyaara
parking garage	مرآب سيارات mir'aab sayyaaraat
parking space	موقف سيارة mawqif sayyaara
part (car-)	جزء juz'
partner	شريك shariik
party	حفلة hafla
passable (road)	عابر 'aabir
passenger	مسافر musaafir
passionfruit	غلال الباشين ghilaal al-bashin
passport	جواز سفر jawaaz safar
passport photo	صورة جواز suurat jawaaz
patient	صابر/مريض mariid / saabir
pay	يدفع yadfa'
pay the bill	دفع الفاتورة daf' al-faatuura
peach	دراق/خوخ khawkh / durraaq
peanut	فستق fustuq
pear	إجاص ijjaas
pearl	لؤلؤ lu'lu'

Word list

15

peas	بازلاء baazillaa'
pedal	دواسة dawwaasa
pedestrian crossing	معبر المترجلين ma'bar al-mutarajjiliin
pedicure	عناية الاقدام 'inaaya al-aqdaam
pen	قلم qalam
pencil	قلم رصاص qalam rasaas
penknife	سكين قلم sikkiin qalam
penis	قضيب qadiib
people	ناس naas
pepper (black)	فلفل أسود fulful aswad
pepper (chilli)	فلفل حار fulful haar
performance	أداء adaa'
perfume	عطر 'itr
perhaps	ربما rubbamaa
period (menstrual)	العادة الشهرية al-'aada ash-shahriyya
permit	رخصة rukhsa
person	شخص shakhs
personal	شخصي shakhsii
pet	حيوان اليف hayawaan aliif
petrol	وقود waquud
petrol station	محطة وقود mahattat waquud
pharmacy	صيدلي saydaliyya
phone	(هاتف) تلفون tilifun (haatif)
phone (verb)	يتصل yatasil
phone booth	كابينة تلفون kabiinat tilifun
phone card	بطاقة تلفون bitaaqat tilifun
phone directory	دليل هاتف daliil haatif
phone number	رقم تلفون (هاتف) raqim tilifun (haatif)
photo	صورة suura
photocopier	آلة النسخ aalat an-nasikh
photocopy	نسخة nuskha
photocopy (verb)	يصور yusawwir
phrasebook	كتاب عبارات kitaab 'ibaaraat
pick up (come to)	(ياخذ) يتسلم yatasallam (ya'khudh)
pick up (go to)	(يوصل) يحمل yahmil (yusil)
picnic	رحلة rihla
pill (contraceptive)	حبوب منع الحمل hubuub man' al-hamal
pills, tablets	حبوب hubuub
pillow	مخدة mikhadda
pillowcase	كيس مخدة kiis mikhadda
pin	دبوس dabbuus
pineapple	اناناس anaanaas

pipe (plumbing)	انبوب	unbuub
pipe (smoking)	غليون	ghalyuun
pipe tobacco	تبغ الغليون	tibgh al-ghalyuun
pity	شفقة	shafaqa
place of interest	اماكن مهمة	amaakin muhimma
plain (simple)	بسيط/صريح	basiit / sariih
plain (not flavored)	بدون نكهة	biduun nukha
plan (intention)	خطة (برنامج)	khutta (barnaanaj)
plan (map)	مستوي	mustawii
plane	طائرة	taa'ira
plant	نبات	nabaat
plaster cast	الجبس الطبي	al-jibs at-tibbii
plastic	بلاستك	blaastik
plastic bag	كيس	kiis
plate	لوح	lawh
platform	منصة	manassa
play (drama)	مسرحية	masrahiyya
play (verb)	يلعب	yal'ab
play golf	لعب الغولف	la'ab al-gulf
playground	منطقة لعب للأطفال	mintaqat la'ib lil-atfaal
playing cards	لعب الورق	la'ib al-waraq
play sports	يلعب رياضة	yal'ab riyaada
play tennis	يلعب التنس	yal'ab at-tinis
pleasant	ممتع	mumti'
please	من فضلك	min fadlik
pleasure	متعة	mut'a
plug (electric)	القابس	al-qaabis
plum	برقوق	barquuq
pocket	جيب	jayb
pocketknife	سكين الجيب	sikkiin al-jayb
point out	يشير الى	yushiir ilaa
poisonous	سام	saam
police	شرطة	shurta
police officer	ضابط شرطة	daabit shurta
police station	مركز الشرطة	markaz as-shurta
pond	بركة	birka
pony	حصان صغير	hisaan saghiir
population	الكثافة السكانية	al-kathaafa as-sukkkaaniyya
pork	لحم خنزير	lahm khinziir
port	ميناء	miinaa'
porter (concierge)	بواب	bawwaab
porter (for bags)	حمال	hammaal

possible	ممكن	mumkin
post (verb)	يرسل بالبريد	yursil bil-bariid
postage	اجرة البريد	ujrat al-bariid
postbox	صندوق بريد	sunduuq bariid
postcard	بطاقة بريدية	bitaaqa bariidiyya
postcode	رمز بريدي	ramz bariidii
post office	مكتب بريد	maktab bariid
postpone	يؤجّل	yu'ajjil
potato	بطاطس	bataatis
potato chips	مقليات بطاطس	maqliyaat bataatis
poultry	دواجن	dawaajin
powdered milk	حليب مجفف	haliib mujaffaf
power outlet	مخرج الكهرباء	makhraj al-kahrabaa'
prawn	جمبري	jambarii
precious metal	معدن ثمين	ma'dan thamiin
precious stone	حجر ثمين	hajar thamiin
prefer	يفضّل	yufaddil
preference	مفضّل	mufaddal
pregnant	حامل	haamil
prescription	وصفة	wasfa
present (gift)	هدية	hadiyya
present (here)	موجود	mawjuud
press (verb)	يضغط	yadghat
pressure	ضغط	daght
price	سعر	si'r
price list	قائمة أسعار	qaa'imat as'aar
print (picture)	يطبع	yatba'
print (verb)	يطبع	yatba'
probably	محتمل	muhtamal
problem	مشكلة	mushkila
profession	مهنة (حرفة)	mihna (harfa)
profit	فائدة (مصلحة)	faa'ida (maslaha)
program	برنامج	barnaamaj
pronounce	يتلفّظ	yatalaffaz
propane	غاز البروبين	ghaaz al-brubiin
pudding	الكعك المحشي	al-ka'ik al-mahshii
pull	يسحب	yashb
pull a muscle	تمطّط العضلة	tamattut al-'adala
pulse	نبض	nabd
pure	نقي	naqii
purify	ينقّي	yunaqqii
purple	بنفسجي	banafsajii

purse (for money)	جزلان	juzlaan
purse (handbag)	حقيبة	haqiiba
push	يدفع	yadfa'
puzzle	لغز	lughz
pyjamas	بيجامة	biijaama

Q

quarter	ربع	rub'
quarter of an hour	ربع ساعة	rub' saa'a
queen	ملكة	malika
question	سؤال	su'aal
quick	سريع	sarii'
quiet	هاديء	haadi'

R

radio	(راديو) مذياع	midhyaa' (radyu)
railroad, railway	سكة القطار	sikkat al-qitaar
rain	مطر	matar
rain (verb)	تمطر	tumtir
raincoat	معطف مطري	mi'taf matarii
rape	اغتصاب	ightisaab
rapid	سريع	sarii'
rash	متهور	mutahawwir
rat	جرذ	juradh
raw	خام	khaam
razor blade	شفرة حلاقة	shafrat hilaaqa
read	يقرأ	yaqra'
ready	جاهز	jaahiz
really	حقا	haqqan
reason	سبب	sabab
receipt	وصل	wasl
reception desk	الاستعلامات	al-isti'laamaat
recipe	وصفة طهوية	wasfa tahwiyya
reclining chair	كرسي هزاز	kursii hazzaz
recommend	ينصح به	yunsah bihi
rectangle	مستطيل	mustatiil
red	احمر	ahmar
red wine	خمر احمر	khamr ahmar
reduction	إنخفاض	inkhifaad
refrigerator	ثلاجة	thallaaja
refund	إعادة مال	i'aadat maal
regards	تحيات	tahiyyat

Word list

15

region	منطقة	mintaqa
registered	مسجل	musajjal
relatives	أقارب	aqaarib
reliable	موثوق	mawthuuq
religion	دين	diin
rent out	يستأجر	yasta'jir
repair	يصلح	yuslih
repairs	ترميم	tarmiim
repeat	يعيد	yu'iid
report (police)	محضر	mahdar
reserve	يحجز	yahjiz
responsible	مسؤول	mas'uul
rest	استراحة	istiraaha
restaurant	مطعم	mat'am
restroom	مرافق صحية	maraafiq sihhiyya
result	نتيجة	natiija
retired	متقاعد	mutaqaa'id
return ticket	تذكرة ذهاب واياب	tadhkira dhahaab wa iyaab
reverse (car)	يرجع الى الوراء	yurji' ilaa al-waraa'
rheumatism	الم المفاصل	alam al-mafaasil
ribbon	شريط	shariit
rice (cooked)	أرز	aruz
rice (grain)	حبوب الأرز	hubuub al-aruz
ridiculous	سخيف	sakhiif
riding (horseback)	راكب	raakib
right (correct)	صحيح	sahiih
right (side)	يمين	yamiin
right of way	أولوية العبور	awlawiyyat al-'ubuur
rinse	يشطف	yashtif
ripe	ناضج	naadij
risk	خطر	khatar
river	نهر	nahir
road	طريق	tariiq
roadway	طريق	tariiq
roasted	محمص	muhammas
rock (stone)	صقرة	saqra
roll (bread)	رغيف	raghiif
roof	سقف	saqf
roof rack	سقف السيارة	saqf as-sayyaara
room	غرفة	ghurfa
room number	رقم الغرفة	raqim al-ghurfa

Word list

15

room service	خدمة الغرفة	<u>kh</u>idmat al-<u>gh</u>urfa
rope	حبل	<u>h</u>abl
route	طريق	<u>t</u>ariiq
rowing boat	زورق تجديف	zawraq tajdiif
rubber	مطاط	ma<u>tt</u>at
rude	غير مهذب	<u>gh</u>ayr muha<u>dh</u>ab
ruins	خراب	<u>kh</u>araab
run	يركض	yarku<u>d</u>
running shoes	حذاء ركض	<u>h</u>idhaa' raki<u>d</u>

S

sad	حزين	<u>h</u>aziin
safe	آمن	aamin
safe (for cash)	خزانة حديدية	<u>kh</u>izaana <u>h</u>adiidiya
safety pin	دبوس الامان	dabbous al-amaan
sail (verb)	يبيع	yabii'
sailing boat	مركب	markab
salad	سلطة	sala<u>t</u>a
sale	بيع	bay'
sales clerk	البائع	al-baa'i'
salt	ملح	mil<u>h</u>
same	نفس/مشابه	mu<u>sh</u>aabih / nafs
sandals	صندل (خف)	<u>s</u>andal (<u>kh</u>uf)
sandy beach	ساحل رملي	saa<u>h</u>il ramlii
sanitary towel	المنديل الصحي	al-mindiil a<u>s</u>-<u>s</u>i<u>hh</u>ii
satisfied	راض	raa<u>d</u>in
Saturday	السبت	as-sabt
sauce	مرق	maraq
saucepan	مقلاة	miqlaat
sauna	حمام بخاري	<u>h</u>ammaam bu<u>kh</u>aarii
say	يقول	yaquul
scald (injury)	حرق	<u>h</u>arq
scales	ميزان	miizaan
scarf (headscarf)	حجاب	<u>h</u>ijaab
scarf (muffler)	قناع	qinaa'
scenic walk	طريق خلاب	<u>t</u>ariiq <u>kh</u>allaab
school	مدرسة	madrasa
scissors	مقص	miqa<u>s</u>
Scotland	اسكتلندا	iskutlandaa
screw	برغي	bur<u>gh</u>ii
screwdriver	مفتاح براغي	mifta<u>h</u> baraa<u>gh</u>ii
scuba diving	الغوص	al-<u>gh</u>aw<u>s</u>

Word list

15

sculpture	فن النحت	fann an-naht
sea	بحر	bahr
seasick	مرض الإبحار	marad al-ibhaar
seat	مقعد	maq'ad
second (in line)	ثاني	thaanii
second (instant)	ثانية	thaaniya
second-hand	مستعمل	musta'mal
sedative	مسكن	musakkin
see	يرى	yaraa
send	يرسل	yursil
sentence	جملة	jumla
separate	منفصل/يفصل	yafsil / munfasil
September	آب	aab
serious	خطير	khatiir
service	خدمة	khidma
service station	محطة بنزين	mahattat banziin
serviette	منديل المائدة	midiil al-maa'ida
sesame oil	زيت السمسم	zayt as-simsim
sesame seeds	سمسم	simsim
set	رزمة/مجموع	majmuua' / ruzma
sew	يخيط	yakhiit
shade	ظل	zil
shallow	ضحل	dahl
shame	عار	'aar
shampoo	شامبو	shambu
shark	قرش	qirsh
shave	يحلق الذقن	yahliq adh-dhaqn
shaver	محلاق كهربائي	mihllaq kahrabaa'ii
shaving cream	معجون حلاقة	ma'juun hilaaqa
sheet	شرشف	sharshaf
shirt	قميص	qamiis
shoe	حذاء	hidhaa'
shoe polish	صبغ حذاء	sibgh hidhaa'
shop, store	متجر/مخزن	makhzan / matjar
shop (verb)	يتسوق	yatasawwaq
shop assistant	بائع	baa'i'
shopping center	(السوق) مركز تسوق	markaz tasawwuq (as-suuq)
shop window	نافذة الدكان	naafidhat ad-dukkan
short	قصير	qasiir
short circuit	دائرة كهربائية	daa'ira karbaa'iyya
shorts (short trousers)	تبان	tubbaan

shorts (underpants)	سروال تحتي قصير	sirwaal tahtii qasiir
shoulder	كتف	katif
show	يري	yurii
shower	دش	dush
shrimp	الروبيان	ruubyaan
shutter (camera)	مصراع	misraa'
shutter (on window)	مصراع	misraa'
sieve	منخل	munkhul
sightseeing	التنزه	at-tanazzuh
sign (road)	علامة	'alaama
sign (verb)	يوقع	yuwaqqi'
signature	توقيع	tawqii'
silence	صمت	samt
silk	سلك	silk
silver	فضة	fidda
simple	بسيط	basiit
single (only one)	واحد	waahid
single (unmarried)	أعزب	a'zab
single ticket	تذكرة واحدة	tadhkirat waahida
sir	سيد	sayyid
sister	أخت	ukht
sit (be sitting)	يجلس	yajlis
sit down	إجلس	ijlis
size	حجم	hajm
skiing	تزلج	tazalluj
skin	جلد	jild
skirt	تنورة	tannuura
sleep	ينام	yanaam
sleeping car	عربة نوم.	'arabat nawm.
sleeping pills	حبوب منومة	hubuub munawwima
sleeve	كم	kum
slip	ينزلق	yanzaliq
slippers	نعال خفيف	nu'aal khafiif
slow	بطيء	batii'
slow train	قطار بطيء	qitaar batii'
small	صغير	saghiir
small change	عملة صغيرة	'umla saghiira
smell	رائحة	raa'iha
smoke	تدخين/دخان	dukhan / tadkhiin
smoked	مدخن	mudakhan
smoke detector	منبه دخان	munabbih dukhaan
snake	حية	hayya

snorkel	أنبوب تنفس مائي unbuub tanaffus maa'ii	
snow	ثلج thalj	
snow (verb)	تثلج tuthlij	
soap	صابون saabuun	
soap powder	مسحوق صابون mashuuq saabuun	
soccer	كرة القدم kurat al-qadam	
soccer match	مباراة كرة قدم mubaaraat kurat qadam	
socket (electric)	مقبس maqbis	
socks	جوارب jawaarib	
soft drink	شراب غير كحولي sharaab ghayr kuhuulii	
sole (of shoe)	قدم qadam	
someone	شخص ما shakhs maa	
sometimes	أحيانا ahyaanan	
somewhere	في مكان ما fii makaanin maa	
son	إبن ibn	
soon	حالا haalan	
sore (painful)	ألم alam	
sore (ulcer)	إلتهاب iltihaab	
sore throat	التهاب الحنجرة iltihaab al-hinjara	
sorry	آسف aasif	
soup	(حساء) شوربة shuurba (hisaa')	
sour	حامض haamid	
south	جنوب januub	
souvenir	تذكار tidhkaar	
soy sauce	صلصة salsa	
spanner, wrench	مفتاح صواميل miftaah sawaamiil	
spare	احتياطي/اضافي ihtiyaatii / idaafii	
spare parts	قطع غيار qita' ghiyaar	
spare tyre	إطار احتياطي itaar ihtiyaatii	
spare wheel	عجلة احتياطي 'ajala ihtiyaatiyya	
speak	يتكلم yatakallam	
special	خاص khaas	
specialist (doctor)	اخصائي akhissaa'ii	
speciality (cooking)	طبخ خاص tabkh khaas	
speed limit	حد السرعة had as-sur'a	
spell	يتلفظ yatalaffaz	
spices	توابل tawaabil	
spicy	حار haar	
splinter	شظية shaziya	
spoon	ملعقة mil'aqa	
sport	رياضة riyaada	
sports center	مركز رياضي markaz riyaadii	

spot (place)	موقع	mawqi'
spot (stain)	نقطة	nuqta
spouse	قرين	qariin
sprain	التواء	iltiwaa'
spring (device)	نابض	naabid
spring (season)	ربيع	rabii'
square (plaza)	ساحة	saaha
square (shape)	مربع	murabba'
square metre	متر مربع	mitr murabba'
squash (game)	الإسكواش	al-iskwaash
squash (vegetable)	هريس	hariis
stadium	ملعب	mal'ab
stain	بقعة	buq'a
stain remover	مزيل البقع	muziil al-buqa'
stairs	درج/سلم	sullam / daraj
stamp	طابع	taaba'
stand (be standing)	قف	qif
stand up	قم	qum
star	نجمة	najma
starfruit	الغلال النجمية	al-ghilaal an-najmiyya
start	يبدأ	yabda'
station	محطة	mahatta
statue	تمثال	timthaal
stay (in hotel)	يقيم	yuqiim
stay (remain)	يبقى	yabqaa
steal	يسرق	yasriq
steam	بخار	bukhaar
steel	فولاذ	fuulaadh
stepfather	زوج الأم	zawj al-um
stepmother	زوجة الأب	zawjat al-ab
steps	خطوات/درجات	darajaat / khutuwaat
sterilize	يعقم	yu'aqqim
sticking plaster	ضماد لاصق	damaad laasiq
sticky tape	شريط لاصق	shariit laasiq
stir-fried	مقلي	maqlii
stitches (in wound)	غرز	ghuraz
stomach (abdomen)	بطن	batn
stomach (organ)	معدة	ma'ida
stomach ache	ألم المعدة	alam al-ma'ida
stomach cramps	مغص في المعدة	maghas fii al-ma'ida
stools	براز	biraaz
stop (bus-)	موقف (محطة)	mawqif (mahatta)

stop (cease)	يتوقف	yatawaqqaf
stop (halt)	يوقف	yuuqif
stopover	متوقف	mutawaqqif
store, shop	مخزن	makhzan
storey	طابق	taabaq
storm	عاصفة	'aasifa
straight	مستقيم	mustaqiim
straight ahead	مباشرة	mubaasharatan
straw (drinking)	مصاصة شرب	massaasat shurb
street	شارع	shaari'
street vendor	بائع متجول	baa'i' mutajawwil
strike (work stoppage)	إضراب	idraab
string	حبل / خيط	khayt / habl
strong	قوي	qawii
study	يدرس / دراسة	diraasa / yadrus
stuffed animal	حيوان محشو	hayawaan mahshuu
stuffing	الحشو	al-hashuu
subtitles	ترجمة الأفلام	tarjamat al-aflaam
succeed	ينجح	yanjah
sugar	سكر	sukkar
suit	بدلة	badla
suitcase	حقيبة	haqiiba
summer	الصيف	as-sayf
sun	شمس	shamsii
sunbathe	حمام شمسي	hammaam shamsii
Sunday	الاحد	al-ahad
sunglasses	نظارات شمسية	nazzaaraat shamsiyya
sunhat	قبعة شمسية	qubba'a shamsiyya
sunrise	شروق الشمس	shuruuq ash-shams
sunscreen	مرهم ضد الشمس	murham did ash-shams
sunset	غروب	ghuruub
sunshade	وقاء من الشمس	waqaa' min ash-shams
sunstroke	ضربة شمس	darbat shams
suntan lotion	مستحضر إسمرار البشرة	mustahdar ismiraar al-bashara
suntan oil	زيت إسمرار البشرة	zayt ismiraar al-bashara
supermarket	السوق المركزية	as-suuq al-markaziyya
surcharge	أجرة اضافية	ujra idaafiyya
surf	الأمواج المتكسرة	al-amwaaj al-mutakassira
surface mail	البريد العادي	al-bariid al-'aadi

surfboard	لوح التزلج على الامواج lawh at-tazalluj 'alaa al-muwaaj
surname	اللقب al-laqab
surprise	مفاجأة mufaaja'a
swallow	يبلع yabla'
swamp	مستنقع mustanqa'
sweat	عرق 'araq
sweater	(بلوز) كلسة kalsa (bluuz)
sweet	حلو huluu
sweetcorn	ذرة حلوة dhura hulwa
swim	يسبح yasbah
swimming costume	زي سباحة zay sibaaha
swimming pool	حوض سباحة hawd sibaaha
swindle	يخدع/خداع khudaa' / yakhda'
switch	مفتاح miftaah
synagogue	معبد يهودي ma'bad yahuudii
syrup	شراب دواء sharaab dawaa'

T

table	منضدة mindada
tablecloth	قماش المنضدة qimaash al-mindada
tablemat	غطاء المنضدة ghitaa' al-mindada
tablespoon	ملعقة طعام milaqa'a ta'aam
table tennis	كرة الطاولة kurat at-taawila
tablets	حبوب hubuub
tableware	أدوات المائدة adawaat al-maa'ida
take (medicine)	يأخذ ya'khudh
take (photo)	يلتقط yaltaqit
take (time)	يستغرق yastaghriq
talk	حديث/يتحدث hadditha / yatahaddath
tall	طويل tawiil
tampon	سدادة siddaada
tanned	مدبوغ madbuugh
tap	حنفية hanafiyya
tap water	ماء الحنفية maa' al-hanafiyya
tape measure	شريط قياس shariit qiyaas
tassel	شرابة shurraaba
taste	طعم ta'am
taste (verb)	يذوق yadhuuq
tax	ضريبة dariiba
tax-free shop	دكان بدون ضريبة dukkaan biduun dariiba
taxi	تاكسي (سيارة اجرة) taaksi (sayyaarat ujra)

taxi stand	موقف تاكسي	mawqif taksii
tea (black)	شاي	<u>sh</u>aay
tea (green)	شاي أخضر	<u>sh</u>aay a<u>kh</u>dar
teacup	كوب	kuub
teapot	أبريق شاي	ibriiq <u>sh</u>aay
teaspoon	ملعقة شاي	mil'aqat <u>sh</u>aay
teat (bottle)	حلمة	<u>h</u>ilma
telephoto lens	عدسة جهاز الفوتغراف	'adasat jihaaz al-futu<u>gh</u>raf
television	تلفزيون	tilifizyuun
telex	تلكس	tiliks
temperature (body)	درجة حرارة	darajat <u>h</u>araara
temperature (heat)	درجة حرارة	darajat <u>h</u>araara
temple	معبد	ma'bad
temporary filling	حشوة مؤقتة	<u>h</u>a<u>sh</u>wa mu'aqqata
tender, sore	ألم	alam
tennis	تنس	tinnis
ten	عشرة	'a<u>sh</u>ara
tent	خيمة	kayma
terminus	نهاية خط الرحلة	nihaayat <u>kh</u>at ar-ri<u>h</u>la
terrace	سطيحة	sa<u>t</u>ii<u>h</u>a
terribly	بفظاعة	bifaza'aa
thank	يشكر	ya<u>sh</u>kur
thank you, thanks	شكرا	<u>sh</u>ukran
thaw	ذوبان	<u>dh</u>awabaan
theatre	مسرح	masra<u>h</u>
theft	سرقة	sariqa
there	هناك	hunaaka
thermometer (body)	ميزان الحرارة	miizaan al-<u>h</u>araara
thermometer (weather)	الترمومتر	at-tirmumitr
thick	سميك	samiik
thief	لص	li<u>s</u>
thigh	فخذ	fa<u>kh</u>i<u>dh</u>
thin (not fat)	نحيف	na<u>h</u>iif
thin (not thick)	رقيق	raqiiq
think (believe)	يظن	ya<u>z</u>un
think (ponder)	يفكر	yufakkir
third (1/3)	ثلث	<u>th</u>ulu<u>th</u>
thirsty	عطشان	'at<u>sh</u>aan
this afternoon	بعد ظهر اليوم	ba'da <u>z</u>uhr al-yawm
this evening	هذا المساء	haa<u>dh</u>aa al-masaa'
this morning	هذا الصباح	haa<u>dh</u>aa a<u>s</u>-sabaah

thread	خيط khayt
throat	حنجرة hunjura
throat lozenges	كراميل الحلق الطبي karaamiil al-halq at-tibbii
thunderstorm	عاصفة رعدية 'aasifa ra'diyya
Thursday	الخميس al-khamiis
ticket (admission)	بطاقة دخول bitaaqat dukhuul
ticket (travel)	تذكرة سفر tadhkira safar
ticket office	مكتب تذاكر maktab tadhaakir
tidy	(ينظم) يرتب yurattib (yunazzim)
tie (necktie)	رباط العنق ribaat al-'unuq
tie (verb)	(يربط) يشد yashud (yarbit)
tights (thick)	سميك samiik
tights (pantyhose)	الرداء المحكم ar-ridaa' al-muhakkam
time (occasion)	مناسبة munaasaba
times (multiplying)	(في) ضارب daarib (fii)
timetable	جدول مواعيد jadwal mawaa'iid
tin (can)	علبة 'ulba
tin opener	مفتاح علب miftaah 'ulab
tip (gratuity)	بقشيش/إكرامية ikraamiyya / baqshiish
tissues	محارم mahaarim
tobacco	تبغ tibgh
today	اليوم al-yawm
toddler	طفل صغير tifl saghiir
toe	إصبع القدم isbi' al-qadam
together	مع بعض maa' ba'd
toilet	التواليت/المرحاض al-mirhaad / at-tuwaaliit
toilet paper	ورق التواليت waraq tuwaaliit
toilet seat	كرسي التواليت kursii at-tuwaaliit
toiletries	مساحيق masaahiiq
tomato	طماطم tamaatim
tomorrow	غدا ghadan
tongue	لسان lisaan
tonight	هذه الليلة haadhihi al-layla
tool	أداة adaat
tooth	سن sin
toothache	ألم أسنان alam asnaan
toothbrush	فرشاة أسنان furshaat asnaan
toothpaste	معجون أسنان ma'juun asnaan
toothpick	عود تظيف الاسنان 'uud tanziif al-asnaan
top	قمة qimma
torch, flashlight	مشعل mish'al
total	مجموع majmuu'

tough	خشن khashin	
tour	رحلة سياحية rihla siyaahiyya	
tour guide	دليل سياحة daliil siyaaha	
tourist class	درجة سياحية daraja siyaahiyy	
tourist information office	مكتب معلومات السياح maktab ma'luumaat as-suyyaah	
tow	(يجر) يسحب yashab (yajur)	
tow cable	سلك سحب silk sahb	
towel	منشف minshaf	
tower	برج burj	
town	(مدينة) بلدة balda (madiina)	
town hall	قاعة البلدية qa'aat al-baladiyya	
toy	لعبة (دمية) lu'ba (dumya)	
traffic	حركة المرور harakat al-muruur	
traffic light	إشارة ضوئية ishaara daw'iyya	
train	قطار qitaar	
train station	محطة القطار mahattat al-qitaar	
train ticket	تذكرة سفر بالقطار tadhkarat safar bil-qitaar	
train timetable	مواعيد القطار mawaa'iid al-qitaar	
translate	يترجم yutarjim	
travel	سفر safar	
travel agent	مكتب سفريات maktab safariyyat	
traveler	مسافر musaafir	
traveler's cheque	شيك سياحي shiik siyaahii	
treatment	معاملة mu'aamala	
triangle	مثلث muthallath	
trim (haircut)	تسريحة tasriiha	
trip	رحلة rihla	
truck	شاحنة shaahina	
trustworthy	موثوق mawthuuq	
try on	قس qis	
tube (of paste)	علبة 'ulba	
Tuesday	الثلاثاء ath-thulaathaa'	
tuna	التن at-tinn	
tunnel	نفق nafaq	
turn off	(اغلق) أطفيء atfi' (aghliq)	
turn on	(افتح) شغل shaghil (iftah)	
turn over	إقلب iqlib	
TV	تلفزيون tilifizyuun	
TV guide	دليل تلفزيون daliil tilifizyon	
tweezers	ملقط صغير milqat saghiir	

twin-bedded	فراش مزدوج	firaa_sh_ muzdawaj
typhoon	إعصار	i'_s_aar
tyre	إطار	i_t_aar
tyre pressure	مستوى الهواء بالإطار	mustawaa al-hawaa' bil-i_t_aar

U

ugly	قبيح	qabii_h_
ulcer	قرحة	qur_h_a
umbrella	مظلة	mi_z_alla
under	تحت	ta_h_ta
underpants	ملابس داخلية	malaabis daa_kh_iliyya
underpass	عبور سفلي	'ubuu_r_ suflii
understand	يفهم	yafham
underwear	ملابس داخلية	malaabis daa_kh_iliyya
undress	يخلع/اخلع	i_kh_la' / ya_kh_la'
unemployed	عاطل عن العمل	'aa_t_il 'an al-'amal
uneven	متعرج	mut'aarrij
university	جامعة	jaami'a
unleaded	بدون رصاص	biduun ra_s_a_s_
up	أعلى (فوق)	a'laa (fawq)
upright	منتصب	munta_s_ib
urgent	ملح (عاجل)	muli_h_ ('aajil)
urgently	بالحاح (عاجلا)	bi'il_h_ah ('aajilan)
urine	بول	bawl
usually	عادة	'aadatan

V

vacate	يترك	yatruk
vacation	عطلة (إجازة)	'utla (ijaaza)
vaccinate	يلقح	yulaqqi_h_
vagina	المهبل	al-mahbal
valid	صالح/قانوني	qaanuunii / saali_h_
valley	وادي	waadii
valuable	ثمين	_th_amiin
valuables	أشياء ثمينة	a_sh_yaa' _th_amiina
van	عربة	'araba
vase	مزهرية	mizhriyya
vegetable	خضروات	_kh_udrawaat
vegetarian	نباتي	nabaatii
vein	عرق/وريد	wariid / 'irq
velvet	مخمل (ناعم)	ma_kh_mal (naa'im)
vending machine	آلة بيع	aalat bay'

venomous	سام saam
venereal disease	مرض تناسلي mara<u>d</u> tanaasulii
vertical	عمودي 'amuudii
via	عبر 'abra
video camera	كاميرة فيديو kamiirat viidiu
video cassette	شريط فيديو <u>sh</u>arii<u>t</u> viidiu
video recorder	مسجل فيديو musajjal viidiu
view	منظر man<u>z</u>ar
village	قرية qarya
visa	تأشيرة/فيزا ta'<u>sh</u>iira (visa)
visit	زيارة/يزور yazuur / ziyaara
visiting time	وقت الزيارة waqt az-ziyaara
vitamins	فيتامينات vitaamiinaat
vitamin tablets	حبوب فيتامينات <u>h</u>ubuub vitaamiinaat
volcano	بركان burkaan
volleyball	الكرة الطائرة al-kura a<u>t</u>-<u>t</u>aa'ira
vomit	يتقيأ yataqayya'

W

wait	ينتظر/إنتظر inta<u>z</u>ir / yanta<u>z</u>ir
waiter	نادل مطعم naadil ma<u>t</u>'am
waiting room	غرفة انتظار <u>gh</u>urfat intizaar
waitress	نادلة في مطعم naadila fii ma<u>t</u>'am
wake up	(افق) ينهض/إنهض inha<u>d</u> / yanha<u>d</u> (afiq)
Wales	ويلز wiiliz
walk (noun)	مشي ma<u>sh</u>ii
walk (verb)	امش/يمشي yam<u>sh</u>ii / im<u>sh</u>i
walking stick	عكاز 'ukaazi
wall	(جدار) حائط <u>h</u>aa'i<u>t</u> (jidaar)
wallet	محفظة نقود mih<u>faz</u>at nuquud
wardrobe	خزانة ثياب <u>kh</u>izaanat <u>th</u>iyaab
warm	دافيء daafi'
warn	يحذر yu<u>h</u>a<u>dh</u>ir
warning	تحذير tah<u>dh</u>iir
wash	يغسل ya<u>gh</u>sil
washing	غسيل <u>gh</u>asiil
washing line	حبل الغسيل <u>h</u>abl al-<u>gh</u>asiil
washing machine	(ماكنة غسيل) غسالة <u>gh</u>assala (maakinat <u>gh</u>asiil)
wasp	دبور dabbuur
watch	ساعة/يشاهد yu<u>sh</u>aahid / sa'aa
water	ماء maa'
waterfall	شلال <u>sh</u>allaal

waterproof	ضد الماء	did al-maa'
water-skiing	تزلج على الماء	tazalluj 'alaa al-maa'
way (direction)	طريق	tariiq
way (method)	طريقة	tariiqa
we	نحن	nahnu
weak	ضعيف	da'iif
wear	يلبس	yalbas
weather	(الجو) الطقس	at-taqs (al-jaw)
weather forecast	الحالة الجوية	al-haala al-jawwiyya
wedding	حفل زفاف	haflu zafaaf
Wednesday	الاربعاء	al-arbi'aa'
week	أسبوع	usbuu'
weekday	يوم دوام	yawm dawaam
weekend	عطلة نهاية الأسبوع	'utlat nihaayat al-usbuu'
weigh	يزن	yazin
weigh-out	يزن	yazin
welcome	اهلا وسهلا	ahlan wa sahlan
well (for water)	جيد	jayyid
well (good)	جيد	jayyid
west	غرب	gharb
wet	رطب (مبلل)	ratib (muballal)
wetsuit	معطف مطري	mi'taf matarii
what?	ماذا؟	maadhaa?
wheel	عجلة	'ajala
wheelchair	كرسي مدولب	kursii mudawlab
when?	متى؟	mataa?
where?	أين؟	ayna?
which?	أي؟	ayy?
white	أبيض	abyad
white wine	نبيذ أبيض	nabiidh abyad
who?	من؟	man?
why?	لماذا؟	limaadhaa?
wide-angle lens	عدسات متسعة الزاوية	'adasaat muttasi'at az-zaawiya
widow	أرملة	armala
widower	ارمل	armal
wife	زوجة	zawja
wind	ريح (رياح)	riih (riyaah)
window (in room)	شباك	shubbaak
window (to pay)	شباك (مكان الدفع)	shubaak (makaan ad-dafi')
windscreen, windshield	الزجاجة الامامية للسيارة	az-zujaaja al-amaamiyya lis-sayyaara

windscreen wiper	ماسحة الزجاجة الأمامية للسيارة maasi<u>h</u>at az-zujaaja al-amaamiyya lis-sayyaara	
wine	نبيذ (كحول) nabii<u>dh</u> (ku<u>h</u>uul)	
winter	شتاء <u>sh</u>itaa'	
wire	سلك silk	
witness	شاهد <u>sh</u>aahid	
woman	أمرأة imra'a	
wonderful	جميل (رائع) jamiil (raa'i')	
wood	خشب <u>kh</u>a<u>sh</u>ab	
wool	صوف <u>s</u>uuf	
word	كلمة kalima	
work	عمل (شغل) 'amal (<u>sh</u>u<u>gh</u>l)	
working day	يوم دوام (يوم عمل) yawm dawaam (yawam 'amal)	
worn	بالي (ممزق) baali (mumazzaq)	
worried	قلق qaliq	
wound	جرح jur<u>h</u>	
wrap	يلف (يغلف) yaluf (yu<u>gh</u>allif)	
wrench, spanner	مفتاح صواميل miftaa<u>h</u> <u>s</u>awaamiil	
wrist	رسغ ris<u>gh</u>	
write	أكتب uktub	
write down	يكتب (يسجل) yaktub (yusajjil)	
writing pad	دفتر للكتابة daftar lilkitaaba	
writing paper	أوراق للكتابة awraaq lilkitaaba	
wrong	خطأ (غلط) <u>kh</u>a<u>t</u>a' (<u>gh</u>al<u>t</u>)	

Y

yarn	خيط <u>kh</u>ay<u>t</u>	
year	سنة sana	
yellow	اصفر a<u>s</u>far	
yes	نعم na'am	
yes please	نعم من فضلك na'am min fa<u>d</u>lik	
yesterday	يوم أمس yawm ams	
you	أنت anta (M) / anti (F)	
youth hostel	مسكن الشباب maskan li<u>sh</u>-<u>sh</u>abaab	

Z

zero	صفر <u>s</u>ifr	
zip	رمز ramz	
zoo	حديقة الحيوانات <u>h</u>adiikatu al-<u>h</u>aywaanaat	
zucchini	كوسة kuusa	

Word list

15

Basic Grammar

There are two genders in Arabic, masculine (m.) and feminine (f.). This applies to verbs, nouns and adjectives.

Verbs

There are two different types of verb in Arabic, depending on their tense/mood: perfective (action complete) and imperfective (action incomplete). Verbs are marked for person, number and gender.

In Arabic first, second and third persons are marked differently in the verb form, e.g. *anna **a**dresu* 'I study,' *anta **ta**dresu* 'you study,' *huwas **ya**dresu* 'he studies.'

Verbs inherently exhibit gender marking in both perfective (past) and imperfective (present) forms. In the perfective form masculine gender is unmarked, whereas feminine gender is shown by a final *t* sound, e.g. *'al-waladu 'akala* 'the boy ate' compared with *'al-bintu 'akalat* 'the girl ate'. In the imperfective form gender is shown by means of prefixes using the *t* and *y* sounds to indicate respectively masculine and feminine genders, e.g. *'al-waladu ya'kulu* 'the boy eats/is eating' compared with *'al-bintu ta'kulu* 'the girl eats/is eating.'

Nouns

There are two types of noun in Arabic. One is known as regular, where the feminine form can be derived from the masculine form, for example:

	Masculine	Feminine
'Student'	*taalib*	*taalib**at***
'Teacher'	*mudarris*	*mudarris**at***
'Driver'	*saa'iq*	*saa'iq**at***

The other class of nouns is irregular, where the masculine and feminine forms do not share the same root and cannot be derived from one another. These should be learned gradually as individual items of vocabulary. Examples of this type of noun are *walad* 'boy,' *bint* 'girl;' *imra'at* 'woman;' *rajul* 'man.'

Note that even non-human nouns are obligatorily marked for gender, e.g. *daar* (f.) 'house,' *madiinat* (f.) 'city,' *balad* (m.) 'country,' *qalam* (m.) 'pen.'

Arabic differentiates between singular, dual and plural numbers, although the dual form is not used frequently. The dual and the regular plural can be derived from the singular form as shown below:

	Root	Singular	Dual	Plural
'Player'	*l-'-b*	*laa'ib*	*laa'ib**aan***	*laa'ib**uun***
'Teacher'	*d-r-s*	*mudarris*	*mudarris**aan***	*mudarris**uun***
'Spectator'	*f-r-j*	*mutafarrij*	*mutafarrij**aan***	*mutafarrij**uun***

The above examples relate to the masculine gender only. Feminine derived nouns take the suffix *–at* in the singular form and replace the masculine plural suffix *–uun* with the feminine plural suffix *–aat*; for example *mudarrisat* 'female teacher' becomes *mudarrisaat* 'female teachers.' The feminine dual form is similar to the masculine form with the exception of the feminine marker *–at* being inserted before the dual suffix, e.g. *mudarris**ataan*** 'two female teachers.'

Definiteness in Arabic is marked in general by means of the article *al-* attached at the beginning of the noun, e.g. *walad* 'a boy,' *al-walad* 'the boy.' However, with a number of consonants, known as the solar consonants, a sound harmony rule means that the final sound of the article is assimilated to the first consonant of the noun, e.g. *sayyaarat* 'a car,' *as-sayyaarat* 'the car.' The consonants to which this applies are *d*, <u>*dh*</u>, <u>*d*</u>, *t*, <u>*t*</u>, <u>*th*</u>, *s*, <u>*sh*</u>, <u>*s*</u>, *z*, <u>*z*</u>, *n*, *l* and *r*.

'Case' refers to the grammatical function assigned to the noun. In Arabic there are three essential case markings—nominative (when the noun is the subject of the sentence), accusative (when the noun is the object of the sentence) and genitive (when the noun is the object of a preposition). Case marking is shown differently depending on the definite or indefinite status of the noun, as shown below for the noun *walad* 'boy:'

	Nominative	Accusative	Genitive
Definite	*al-walad**u***	*al-walad**a***	*al-walad**i***
Indefinite	*walad**un***	*walad**an***	*walad**in***

Adjectives

Adjectives tend to go after the noun to which they refer. They must agree with the noun they accompany in gender (masculine or feminine), number (singular, dual or plural) and case (nominative, accusative or genitive), e.g. ***al**-walad**u** **an**-najiib**u** naja<u>h</u>a* 'the studious boy passed (the exam);' *qaabalt**u** **al**-walad**a** **an**-najiib**a*** 'I met the studious boy.'

Possessive adjectives

Possessive adjectives agree in gender and number with the noun to which they relate (the owner), as in English. They cannot be used in conjunction with the definite article. The following examples using the word *kitaab* 'book' illustrate the way possessives are marked in Arabic.

*kitaab-**ii***	'my book'
*kitaabu-**ka***	'your (m. sing.) book'
*kitaabu-**ki***	'your (f. sing.) book'
*kitaabu-**hu***	'his book'
*kitaabu-**ha***	'her book'
*kitaabu-**kumaa***	'your (dual) book'
*kitaabu-**humaa***	'their (dual) book'
*kitaabu-**naa***	'our book'
*kitaabu-**kum***	'your (m. pl.) book'
*kitaabu-**kunna***	'your (f. pl.) book'
*kitaabu-**hum***	'their (m. pl.) book'
*kitaabu-**hunna***	'their (f. pl.) book'

Personal pronouns

Since verb endings (*-tu, -ta, -ti, -tum,* etc) can be sufficient to indicate who is doing the action, personal pronouns are not always used. However, to avoid confusion, you should use them. The Arabic personal pronouns are:

I	*anaa*
you (m. sing.)	*anta*
you (f. sing.)	*anti*
he	*huwa*
she	*huya*
you (dual)	*antumaa*
they (dual)	*umaa*
we	*nahnu*
you (m. pl.)	*antum*
you (f. pl.)	*antunna*
they (m.)	*hum*
they (f.)	*hunna*

Forming questions

The easiest way of asking a question in Arabic is by using one of a number of question words at the beginning of the statement or phrase. However, the type of question word used depends on the sentence or phrase itself (similar to English in its distinction between 'do/does' and 'what/why,' etc). The following are examples of the most frequent question words: **maa** *haadha* 'what's this?;' **ayyat** *imra'a* 'which lady?;' **ay** *rajul* 'which man?;' **man** *anta* 'who are you?'

Examples of turning a declarative sentence (statement) into an interrogative one (question):

akala al-waladu 'the boy ate'
> —> **hal** *akala al-waladu* 'did the boy eat?'

kharajat al-bintu 'the girl left'
> —> **limaadhaa** *kharajat al-bintu* 'why did the girl leave?'

habatat at-taa'ira 'the plane landed'
> —> **mataa** *habatat at-taa'ira* 'when did the plane land?'

ishtaraa qamiis 'he bought a shirt'
> —> **ayna** *ishtaraa qamiis* 'where did he buy a shirt?'

Forming negative sentences

As with forming questions, negation is expressed differently for nominal as opposed to verbal sentences.

When negating nominal and adjectival phrases, *laysa* and its variants are used as shown below. The nominal negation word *laysa* is always inserted after the pronoun or noun to which it refers, e.g. **lastu** ghaadiban 'not I angry,' i.e. 'I am not angry.'

Here are the various forms of *laysa* with the main pronouns:

anaa	I	*lastu*
anta	you (m. sing.)	*lasta*
anti	you (f. sing.)	*lasti*
huwa	he	*laysa*
hiya	she	*laysat*
nahnu	we	*lasnaa*
antum	you (m. pl.)	*astum*
antunna	you (f. pl.)	*lastunna*
hum	they (m.)	*laysuu*

There are four verbal negation words used to negate verbal actions in the present, past and the future respectively. These are shown in the following examples:

laa	present	**laa** a<u>sh</u>rab	I don't write.
lan	future	**lan** <u>sh</u>rab	I won't drink.
lam	past	**lam** a<u>sh</u>rab	I did not drink.
maa	past/continuing	**maa** <u>sh</u>aribtu	I have not drunk.